SOVEREIGNTY

≒ A PLAY ≒

MARY KATHRYN NAGLE

NORTHWESTERN UNIVERSITY PRESS

EVANSTON, ILLINOIS

Northwestern University Press
www.nupress.northwestern.edu

Printed in the United States of America

10 9 8 7 6 5 4 3 2 1

CAUTION: Professionals and amateurs are hereby warned that performance of *Sovereignty: A Play* is subject to payment of a royalty. It is fully protected under the copyright laws of the United States of America, and of all countries covered by the International Copyright Union (including the Dominion of Canada and the rest of the British Commonwealth), and of all countries covered by the Pan-American Copyright Convention, the Universal Copyright Convention, the Berne Convention, and of all countries with which the United States has reciprocal copyright relations. All rights, including without limitation professional and amateur stage rights, motion picture, recitation, lecturing, public reading, radio broadcasting, television, video or sound recording, all other forms of mechanical, electronic and digital reproduction, transmission and distribution, such as CD, DVD, the Internet, private and file-sharing networks, information storage and retrieval systems, photocopying, and the rights of translation into foreign languages are strictly reserved. Particular emphasis is placed upon the matter of readings, permission for which must be secured from the Author's agent in writing.

Inquiries concerning rights should be addressed to William Morris Endeavor Entertainment, LLC, 11 Madison Avenue, 18th Floor, New York, N.Y. 10010. Attn: Michael Finkle.

LIBRARY OF CONGRESS
CATALOGING-IN-PUBLICATION DATA

Names: Nagle, Mary Kathryn, author.
Title: Sovereignty : a play / Mary Kathryn Nagle.
Description: Evanston : Northwestern University Press, 2020.
Identifiers: LCCN 2019024777 | ISBN 9780810141407 (trade paperback) | ISBN | 9780810141414 (ebook)
Subjects: LCSH: Cherokee Indians—Oklahoma—Drama. | Indians of North America—Criminal justice system—Drama.
Classification: LCC PS3614.A465 S68 2020 | DDC 812.6—dc23
LC record available at https://lccn.loc.gov/2019024777

SOVEREIGNTY

CONTENTS

ACKNOWLEDGMENTS

The playwright wishes to thank Cherokee Nation citizen John Ross for his work on the Cherokee language translations for the play. She would also like to acknowledge the life and legacy of Dr. Duane King, one of the greatest friends the Cherokee have ever had. Without his support, research, and hard work, the telling of this story would not have been possible. Wado!

PRODUCTION HISTORY

The world premiere of *Sovereignty* in Washington, D.C., took place at Arena Stage on January 12, 2018, with artistic direction by Molly Smith. Edgar Dobie was the executive producer. Scenic design was by Ken MacDonald, lighting design by Robert Wierzel, sound design by Ed Littlefield, and projection design by Mark Holthusen. Costume design was by Linda Cho; wig design was by Jon Aitchison. Fight direction was by Lewis Shaw, and the production stage manager was Susan R. White. The cast was as follows:

John Ridge	Kalani Queypo
Sarah Ridge Polson	Kyla García
Major Ridge/Roger Ridge Polson	Andrew Roa
Elias Boudinot/Watie	Jake Hart
John Ross/Jim Ross	Jake Waid
Andrew Jackson/Ben	Joseph Carlson
Samuel Worcester/Mitch	Michael Glenn
Sarah Bird Northrup/Flora Ridge	Dorea Schmidt
White Chorus Man	Todd Scofield

Sovereignty was originally commissioned by Drs. Elliot and Lily Gardner Feldman and BakerHostetler as part of Arena Stage's Women's Voices Power Play Cycle. Additional Commissioning support provided by the Virginia B. Toulmin Foundation's Women Playwrights Commissioning Program.

SOVEREIGNTY

CHARACTERS

Sovereignty takes place in the early 1800s and in the present. We transition back and forth in time fluidly and quickly; consequently, the costumes and set should not be fully realized in either time period. The worlds coexist, since at any given moment we are a reflection of our past and present, and we project that into our future.

Nine actors (seven men, two women) play all the roles:

1800s / *The Present*

John Ridge
Sarah Ridge Polson
Major Ridge / *Roger Ridge Polson (Sarah's father)*
Elias Boudinot / *Watie (Sarah's brother)*
John Ross / *Jim Ross*
Andrew Jackson / *Ben (Sarah's fiancé)*
Samuel Worcester / *Mitch (Sarah's childhood friend)*
Sarah Bird Northrup / *Flora Ridge*
White Chorus Man: Governor Forsyth, Georgia Guard, William Wirt, Reverend Schermerhorn / *Drunk Man, Bartender*

1800s

Major Ridge. Given the title "Major" after fighting with General Andrew Jackson in the War of 1812, Major Ridge was an influential leader in Cherokee Nation politics from the 1810s until his assassination in 1839. He served many years as the speaker of Cherokee Nation Council and as Chief John Ross's assistant, until the divide that takes place in this play. He and his son were among those who signed the Treaty of New Echota on December 29, 1835, which became the basis for the forcible removal known as the Trail of Tears.

John Ridge. The son of Major Ridge, John Ridge was an influential leader in Cherokee Nation from the 1820s to his assassination in 1839. He served as clerk to Cherokee Nation National Committee (the Council), and, with his father, signed the Treaty of New Echota.

Sarah Bird Northrup. John Ridge's wife, the daughter of a schoolmaster in Cornwall, Connecticut. She is non-Indian.

Elias Boudinot. His father was Major Ridge's brother. Elias Boudinot went to Cornwall for school with his cousin John Ridge and then returned home to Cherokee Nation and became the first editor of the *Cherokee Phoenix*, the first printed paper of an Indian Nation. He also signed the Treaty of New Echota in 1835.

John Ross. Chief of Cherokee Nation from 1828 until his death in the 1860s, John Ross led Cherokee Nation through significant turmoil, including the removal and the Civil War. He is revered by Cherokees today as one of the most important Cherokee leaders of all time.

Andrew Jackson. An American soldier and statesman who served as president of the United States from 1829 to 1837, Andrew Jackson believed Indians were an inferior race that should disappear from the face of the earth.

Samuel Worcester. A white man who went to live in Cherokee Nation as a missionary, Samuel Worcester worked with Elias Boudinot to translate the Bible into Cherokee. His arrest in 1832 sparked one of the most significant Supreme Court cases in United States history, *Worcester v. Georgia.*

THE PRESENT

Sarah Ridge Polson. A direct descendant of Major Ridge, and of John Ridge and Sarah Bird Northrup, Sarah is a graduate of Yale Law School and a citizen of Cherokee Nation who returns home to Cherokee Nation after a long absence.

Roger (Ridge) Polson. Also a direct descendant of Major Ridge and the others, Roger is the father of Sarah Ridge Polson and Watie Polson.

Watie. He is Sarah Ridge Polson's brother and Roger (Ridge) Polson's son. He works for the Cherokee Nation police force.

Jim Ross. A direct descendant of John Ross. Jim is Sarah Ridge Polson's boss in the attorney general's office.

Ben. A Special Victims Unit police officer in present-day Oklahoma. He becomes Sarah Ridge Polson's fiancé. He is non-Indian.

Mitch. A lawyer, non-Indian, living in Oklahoma. Childhood friend of Sarah and Watie.

Flora. Also a direct descendant of Major Ridge and a citizen of Cherokee Nation, Flora runs the family cemetery where Major Ridge and John Ridge are buried, just a few hundred yards from where John was murdered. Sarah and Watie are her niece and nephew, and Roger is her brother.

ACT 1

SCENE 1

[*Present day. The Ridge Polson Cemetery.* SARAH RIDGE POLSON *stands before* JOHN RIDGE'S *grave, with a jar of dirt.* SARAH *opens the jar and pours the dirt over the grave.* FLORA *enters.*]

FLORA: Haven't seen you here since we buried your mom.

SARAH: I'm moving back.

FLORA: To Cherokee Nation?

SARAH: To Tahlequah.

FLORA: I thought you were in Chicago.

SARAH: I was. But now I've applied for a job. Here. With the attorney general's office.

FLORA: Rosses control that office.

SARAH: I might work for one.

FLORA: How the hell you gonna convince him to hire a Ridge?

SARAH: I don't have to tell him.

FLORA: What if he finds out?

SARAH: He's not going to find out—

FLORA: The moment he finds out you're a Ridge, he'll do whatever he can to undermine you, your work, and your reputation. The day you trust a Ross is the day they kill you.

[Beat.]

FLORA [points to the jar]: What's in the jar?

SARAH: On my drive here I took a little detour through Georgia—

FLORA: To New Echota?

SARAH: I visited Worcester's house, Elias Boudinot's house, the old Supreme Court building, and then I stopped at Sarah and John's. I thought I'd bring a little bit of their old home to their home here, but I can't find Sarah. I thought she must be next to John Ridge. But she's not. I've checked each row like ten times. Up and down and back again. And I can't find her.

FLORA: She's in Arkansas.

SARAH: She's buried in Arkansas?

FLORA: You didn't know.

SARAH: I never looked for her—

FLORA: You're named after her. She's your namesake. *Sarah* Bird Northrup.

SARAH: I know her name.

FLORA: You just don't know where she's buried.

SARAH: No one talks in this family—

FLORA: You know where John is. You visit him.

SARAH: My mom, grandma, Uncle Buck, my whole family's buried ten feet away from him.

FLORA: After they killed John, she took the kids and left. She never came back.

SARAH: Grandma never spoke of Sarah.

FLORA: Her story is the saddest.

SCENE 2

[*Cherokee Nation Hard Rock Casino, Catoosa, Oklahoma.* MITCH *and* BEN *sit at the bar drinking beers.*]

MITCH: Only once.

BEN: Mmm-hmm.

MITCH: I'm serious.

BEN: You're full of shit.

MITCH: She was hot.

BEN: Lemme see.

MITCH: What?

BEN: A photo.

MITCH: That was eighteen years ago.

BEN: Come on man, third grade doesn't count.

MITCH: Fifth. I remember because she was in sixth—

BEN: So you like older women.

MITCH: One year older. We went out.

BEN: Where?

MITCH: It's a phrase. You know, "went out."

BEN: I said have you ever *dated* an Indian—

MITCH: She kissed me. By the swings. At recess.

[WATIE *enters, in his tribal police uniform, making his rounds on the casino floor.*]

WATIE: Been an exciting night so far.

MITCH: Yeah?

WATIE: I just got called to the northwest lot to assist a ninety-two-year-old in a fender bender with a tree.

MITCH: How do you get into a fender bender with a tree?

WATIE: Exactly. Not to mention the bleached-blond twenty-four-carat-diamond lady puking all over a slot machine in the east wing, or the guy on nine who set his mustache on fire—

MITCH: Take a load off. I'll get you a beer.

WATIE: Can't. Got ten and I'm back on.

BEN [*extends his hand to shake* WATIE'S]: Hey, I'm Ben.

WATIE: Watie.

[*They shake hands.*]

MITCH: Sorry I forget my friends don't know each other. Watie, this is Ben. Ben this is Watie. Watie here went to school with me—

WATIE: We go back—

MITCH: Way back—

WATIE: Like fifth-grade back.

BEN: Any friend of Mitch is a friend of mine.

WATIE: Likewise.

[DRUNK MAN *enters, making a beeline for the bar.*]

DRUNK MAN [*to* WATIE]: Outta my way.

WATIE: Excuse me.

DRUNK MAN: You deaf? I said outta my way.

MITCH: Hey buddy, this guy here's police. You're talking to a cop.

DRUNK MAN: I don't care if I'm talkin' to Jesus. Ima order a drink.

WATIE: How much have you had to drink tonight, sir?

DRUNK MAN: Tell this redskin outta my way.

[BEN *stands up.*]

WATIE [*to* BEN]: I got this.

BEN: He's really drunk.

WATIE: They usually are. [*To* DRUNK MAN] Sir, I think you've had too much to drink.

DRUNK MAN: I ain't had enough.

WATIE: I'm gonna have to ask you to leave.

DRUNK MAN: I got a right to be here.

MITCH [*to* WATIE]: Do you need us to move?

WATIE [*to* MITCH]: You're fine. [*To* DRUNK MAN] I'm gonna give you to the count of three, and then you'll be escorted out. One.

DRUNK MAN: Fuck you.

WATIE: Two.

DRUNK MAN: You wanna go?

MITCH: Watie—

WATIE: Three—

DRUNK MAN: Arghhhh!

[*Groans and general sounds of agonized, drunken fighting.* DRUNK MAN *lunges at* WATIE, *taking him down.* WATIE, *aware that he has no jurisdiction, isn't quite sure how to react.* DRUNK MAN *is on top of* WATIE *and prepares to land another punch when* BEN *pulls him off and places cuffs on* DRUNK MAN.]

BEN: Sir, you're under arrest. You have the right to remain silent.

WATIE: You're police?

MITCH: Ben's with the state.

BEN: Special Victims Unit.

[BEN *flashes his badge.*]

DRUNK MAN: Fuck you man!

BEN: Anything you say can and will be used against you—

WATIE: You can't arrest him.

DRUNK MAN: You can't arrest me!

WATIE: This is Cherokee Nation.

DRUNK MAN: Fuck Cherokee Nation.

BEN: Shit. You're right. We don't have jurisdiction. [BEN *backs off*] He's all yours.

WATIE: I can't.

DRUNK MAN: Lemme go!

BEN [*to* DRUNK MAN]: Shut up! [*To* WATIE] What do you mean you can't?

WATIE: I'm tribal police.

BEN: So arrest him.

DRUNK MAN: Fuckin' hell man!

WATIE: I can't arrest a non-Native who attacks a Native.

BEN: Says who?

WATIE: The U.S. Supreme Court.

DRUNK MAN: Yeah. I got rights!

BEN: So you're telling me no one has jurisdiction?

WATIE: The Feds. They can arrest him.

BEN: But they aren't here.

WATIE: They never are.

DRUNK MAN: Can I go now?

[BEN *releases* DRUNK MAN, *who taunts* BEN *and* WATIE *and then exits.*]

BEN: Do you think he'll sue me?

WATIE: You should sue *him*.

BEN: I arrested him. Without sufficient authority. Isn't that like, a constitutional right violation?

WATIE: I dunno. Mitch is the lawyer. I'm just police.

MITCH: I do family law. I don't know shit about the Constitution. I mean, I know we got one—

WATIE [*in pain*]: Ahhhh.

MITCH: Take it easy now.

BEN: Does it hurt?

MITCH: You're gonna have a black eye.

WATIE: I'm fine.

[SARAH *enters.*]

SARAH: They said you were making rounds, but I should've known you'd be at the bar— [*She sees his face*] Oh my god, Watie!

WATIE: I'm fine.

SARAH: What happened?

MITCH: He was attacked.

WATIE: I wasn't attacked.

BEN: By a drunk white dude.

WATIE: He got a few punches in, and then we let him go.

SARAH: Did you call the Feds?

WATIE: I generally don't do things that waste my time.

SARAH: You need to report this.

WATIE: Name one time the Feds actually showed up.

SARAH: I'll get you some ice—

WATIE: I'm fine—

SARAH: You're bleeding.

WATIE [*picks up a bar napkin*]: I have this napkin.

MITCH [*to* SARAH]: I didn't know you were in town.

SARAH: Hi Mitch.

WATIE: She's moving back.

SARAH: Speaking of which, where are your keys?

WATIE: Under the mat. I left you a key—

SARAH: It doesn't unlock your door.

WATIE: Oh shit, yeah. That's the toolshed.

SARAH: I'm not sleeping in the toolshed.

WATIE: No, probably not.

MITCH: You're moving back?

SARAH: Yeah.

MITCH: To Jay?

WATIE: To Tahlequah. If she can get a job.

SARAH: I'm interviewing to work in the attorney general's office.

WATIE: She wants to work for a Ross.

SARAH: I want to work for the Cherokee Nation.

MITCH: They'll let you do that?

SARAH: I don't have to tell him I'm a Ridge.

WATIE: Just hide who you are. It's cool, no one will ever know.

SARAH: Do you tell everyone you meet you're a Ridge?

BEN: What's a "Ridge"?

SARAH: See, your friend here doesn't know you're a Ridge.

WATIE: I met him like five minutes ago.

SARAH: So he's a complete stranger.

MITCH: He's *my* friend.

WATIE: And he saved my ass.

BEN: I tried. But I couldn't arrest the guy. I'm police. SVU.

MITCH: Special Victims Unit.

SARAH: I know SVU.

BEN: I was working, you know, in Houston—

MITCH: And they recruited him—the state—to come here, 'cause when it comes to SVU, he's the best.

BEN [*to* SARAH]: I'm a detective.

SARAH [*to* BEN]: Do you have a name?

BEN [*extends his hand to* SARAH]: Ben.

SARAH: Nice to meet you, Ben. I'm Sarah.

BEN: Sarah. That, you know, definitely has a ring to it.

[*They stare at one another.*]

BEN: So crazy to be standing there—you know, two sets of police, and neither one of us could do anything.

SARAH: Because of *Oliphant.*

BEN: An elephant?

MITCH AND SARAH: *Oliphant.*

MITCH: Supreme Court case.

WATIE: Oh no. Two attorneys in the same room.

SARAH: In 1978 the Supreme Court said Tribes can no longer exercise criminal jurisdiction over non-Indians who come onto tribal lands and commit a crime.

BEN: That's just wrong.

SARAH: Tell that to your United States Supreme Court.

BEN: You don't like the court?

SARAH: I respect it.

BEN: So you're like a Catholic that hates the Vatican.

SARAH: It's hard to worship an institution that always decides against you.

BEN: You've never won a case?

SARAH: *Worcester v. Georgia.*

WATIE: We won a case in 1822.

SARAH: Thirty-two.

WATIE: Thirty-two, excuse me.

BEN: Rooster v. Georgia?

SARAH: Yes, but pronounced "wooster."

BEN: Indians have weird names.

WATIE: Worcester was white.

SARAH: We won that case. And we've lost ever since.

BEN: So you're telling me that because of this Elephant case, I could steal your car, I could steal your yoga mat—

SARAH: I don't do yoga.

BEN: But if you did—

SARAH: You could set my house on fire, graffiti our courthouse, kill someone, basically do whatever you want, and Cherokee Nation could never prosecute you. But, if Cherokee Nation were to actually get off its butt and implement VAWA, we could prosecute domestic violence crimes perpetrated by non-Indians.

WATIE: Va what?

SARAH: Violence Against Women Act. You don't know about the Violence Against Women Act?

WATIE: I'm a man.

SARAH: Just six years ago, Congress reauthorized the Violence Against Women Act *with* a tribal jurisdiction provision in it.

WATIE: You lost me at authorized. Can I make a suggestion? Skip anything above two syllables.

BEN: VA-WA, that works.

SARAH: In VAWA, Congress restored a piece of our criminal jurisdiction. The criminal jurisdiction that *Oliphant* took away.

WATIE: Jur-is-dic-shun. You lost me at dick.

SARAH: You know jurisdiction.

WATIE: I know we don't have it. Over white guys.

SARAH: And I'm telling you that VAWA restored it. A piece of it.

WATIE: Oh. Wow.

SARAH: Yeah.

WATIE: Why didn't you tell me that in the first place?

SARAH: I swear. Sometimes I want to hit you.

MITCH: You're not the only one.

BEN [*to* SARAH]: Are you this passionate about everything in life?

WATIE: All right, I'm back on.

MITCH: Already?

WATIE: My ten minutes are up. Gentlemen, I'd say it's been a
    pleasure, but—

SARAH: Do you need to see a doctor? You know, get checked out?

WATIE: Why?

SARAH: You were hit in the face.

WATIE: I'll be fine.

SARAH: Watie!

[WATIE *goes to exit.*]

SARAH: The key. To your apartment.

WATIE: Look in the mailbox. Mitch, good to see you—

MITCH: See you around, man.

BEN: Nice to meet you.

WATIE: Thanks for saving my ass.

BEN: I didn't do anything.

WATIE: You did more than I could.

[WATIE *exits.*]

MITCH: OK, well, it's late and—

SARAH: It's a drive. You know, back to Jay.

MITCH: It sure is. Good to see you, Sarah.

SARAH: Don't be a stranger. I live here now.

[MITCH *starts to exit.*]

MITCH: Ben.

BEN: Huh?

MITCH: I'm your ride.

BEN: Oh, yeah. Right. [*To* SARAH] Hey, I gotta go.

SARAH: OK. Yeah . . . see you around.

BEN: Hey, uh, you wanna get dinner?

SARAH: Oh, I'm good. Just ate.

MITCH: He's asking you on a date.

SARAH: Oh.

BEN: It's cool, you're a busy woman—

MITCH: He knows you're a big deal.

BEN: You've got cases to win and—

SARAH: Yes.

BEN: Yes?

MITCH: Yes, she'll go to dinner with you.

SARAH: I'd love to.

MITCH: OK, bye.

[MITCH *exits.* BEN *looks at* SARAH. *He exits.*]

SCENE 3

[SARAH *enters the Cherokee Nation attorney general's office.* JIM ROSS *sits at his desk.*]

JIM ROSS: Sarah Polson.

SARAH: That's me.

JIM ROSS: Very impressive résumé.

SARAH: Thank you.

JIM ROSS: And you think you want to work in the attorney general's office?

SARAH: I know I do.

JIM ROSS: This isn't Yale, you know.

SARAH: Sure—

JIM ROSS: We don't sit around drinking lattes and debating what Thomas Jefferson meant when he said some shit back in 1804.

SARAH: He called us "merciless savages" in the Declaration of Independence. I think we all know what that means. We don't need to debate it.

JIM ROSS: What'd you study? In law school.

SARAH: The law.

JIM ROSS: Right. What classes did you take?

SARAH: Just, you know, the regular classes—

JIM ROSS: Did you take Indian law?

SARAH: I did not.

JIM ROSS: You want to practice Indian law but you never studied it.

SARAH: Yale didn't offer it.

JIM ROSS: So you studied their Constitution but didn't study ours.

SARAH: I don't need to study our Constitution. I know it.

JIM ROSS: Which one.

SARAH: All of them—

JIM ROSS: All of them.

SARAH: 1999; September 6, 1839; 1827—

JIM ROSS: You're a citizen?

SARAH: I'm enrolled.

JIM ROSS: But you've never lived in Tahlequah.

SARAH: I was born in Jay.

JIM ROSS: But you've never lived there—

SARAH: I grew up there.

JIM ROSS: But as an adult. You've never lived there.

SARAH: You're right. I've never lived there as an adult.

JIM ROSS: And you're sure now, after living in [*reading from her résumé*] New Haven, New York, Chicago, after living in all those places, you're ready to drive ten miles to Walmart just to buy shampoo, eat tater tots at Sonic, and connect to wi-fi periodically. If you're lucky. This is Tahlequah. We don't have Starbucks.

SARAH: I want to come home.

[*Beat.*]

JIM ROSS: Forgive me, it's just, I can't afford to hire someone that's gonna quit after two weeks—

SARAH: You think I would quit?

JIM ROSS: You might, after you've been here—

SARAH: I've never quit anything in my life.

JIM ROSS [*reading from her résumé*]: Southern District of New York, clerkship; Judge Posner, Seventh Circuit, clerkship—with a résumé like this, you should be clerking on the Supreme Court. Not working in Tahlequah.

SARAH: In the entire history of the Supreme Court, there'd never been a single Native law clerk until last year. Gorsuch hired the first one.

JIM ROSS: Why not make it two?

SARAH: I applied to clerk on the Supreme Court. Three years in a row. Didn't even get an interview.

[*Beat.*]

I want to serve my nation.

JIM ROSS: If you could accomplish one thing while you work in this office, what would it be?

SARAH: One of the perks of being a student at Yale, besides the lattes and enlightened discussions of what our "founding fathers" meant, is that your professors are connected. You know, to high-ups in the government. One of my professors had come from the DOJ. And she came to me one day and said, "Hey, do you want a ticket to the VAWA signing ceremony—"

JIM ROSS: VAWA?

SARAH: Violence Against Women Act—

JIM ROSS: I know what VAWA is.

SARAH: I was there. On March 7, 2013, when the president signed VAWA into law. I watched Diane Millich share her story—

JIM ROSS: I've read her story, in the *New York Times*.

SARAH: I watched her introduce the president.

JIM ROSS: You want to work on VAWA.

SARAH: I want Cherokee Nation to implement it.

JIM ROSS: We just did. Council voted sixteen-zero to implement VAWA 904—

SARAH: They agreed to implement VAWA?

JIM ROSS: Based on a resolution I drafted and presented.

SARAH: To me, VAWA is no different than treaty signing.

JIM ROSS: Yes!

SARAH: It's a modern-day treaty from one sovereign to another.

JIM ROSS: Exactly!

SARAH: Like the Treaty of New Echota—

JIM ROSS: What?

SARAH: I'm just making a comparison—

JIM ROSS: We don't talk about that treaty.

SARAH: Who's "we"?

JIM ROSS: Me, everyone, the entire Cherokee Nation. Traitors signed that treaty—

SARAH: The Ridges signed that treaty.

JIM ROSS: Like I said, traitors signed that treaty. They caused the Trail of Tears.

SARAH: Do you know any Ridges?

JIM ROSS: Never met one. They don't exist. I mean, they might exist elsewhere. But they aren't here, in Cherokee Nation. They signed the treaty, and then they left. Never came back. I heard one lived in California. Maybe Seattle. I don't know, and I don't care.
   Look, sorry. I'm a Ross. You know, Jim *Ross*. John Ross was my grandfather's great-grandfather. I'm a direct descendant. So please, never ever talk to me about that treaty.

SARAH: Understood.

JIM ROSS: But what you're saying about treaties is right—

SARAH: After they've been ratified by the Senate, they're the "supreme law of the land"—

JIM ROSS: I want you to come with me.

SARAH: Where?

JIM ROSS: D.C. The Department of Justice meets with every Tribe that implements VAWA 904. So now they want to meet with us. And I want you to prepare my talking points—

SARAH: For the DOJ?

JIM ROSS: We leave on Monday.

SARAH: Does this mean?

JIM ROSS: You're hired.

SCENE 4

[*Shift to the past. 1820s.* JOHN RIDGE *enters, a pencil tucked tightly between his lips, his legs immobile. He pulls himself across the floor using his arms only, in his small room in the Northrups' home in Cornwall, Connecticut. He is ill and has lost the ability to walk. His crutches lean against the bed. He arrives at the bed and attempts to pull himself up. He fails.*]

[ELIAS BOUDINOT *enters, carrying several books. He stops when he sees* JOHN RIDGE.]

JOHN RIDGE [*taking the pencil out of his mouth*]: I dropped my pencil.

ELIAS BOUDINOT [*putting the books down on the bedside table*]: Let me help you—

JOHN RIDGE: I can do this.

[JOHN RIDGE *puts the pencil back between his lips and struggles again to pull himself into bed. He fails. Beat. He looks to* ELIAS BOUDINOT. *Without saying a word,* ELIAS BOUDINOT *picks him up and places him in his bed.*]

ELIAS BOUDINOT: We moved on to Cicero.

JOHN RIDGE: Already?

ELIAS BOUDINOT: Teacher skipped ahead. Said Cicero's the most important of all the Roman philosophers, so we should study him first. You do your lessons for Latin?

[JOHN RIDGE *nods*.]

ELIAS BOUDINOT: Let me know if you have any questions.

[ELIAS BOUDINOT *turns to exit*.]

JOHN RIDGE: Buck. Before you leave, could you—

ELIAS BOUDINOT: Elias. I changed my name.

JOHN RIDGE: Sure, but—

ELIAS BOUDINOT: I want you to call me by my name.

JOHN RIDGE: A name that truly isn't your name.

ELIAS BOUDINOT: Elias Boudinot was a delegate to the Continental Congress; he was appointed by President Washington to—

JOHN RIDGE: You admire him.

ELIAS BOUDINOT: So what if I do?

JOHN RIDGE: Gallegina Uwatie. That's what your parents named you.

ELIAS BOUDINOT: Elias Boudinot sponsored me. He got me into this school.

JOHN RIDGE: I had a sponsor to come here—I had to—but I never took his name.

ELIAS BOUDINOT [*brandishing the Bible*]: Psalm 147:3. "He heals the brokenhearted—"

JOHN RIDGE: Not now.

ELIAS BOUDINOT [*replacing the Bible on the bedside table*]: Professing your faith in the Christian church could make your love for the schoolmaster's daughter a bit more palatable.

JOHN RIDGE: You will never hear me profess a faith I do not possess.

ELIAS BOUDINOT: Everyone keeps asking me, Elias, when will your cousin John accept the Lord our Christ into his heart?

JOHN RIDGE: When they accept the Indian into theirs.

[*Beat.*]

ELIAS BOUDINOT: What did the doctor say?

JOHN RIDGE: He doesn't know.

ELIAS BOUDINOT: But you will walk again.

JOHN RIDGE: He said I might never.

[SARAH BIRD NORTHRUP *enters, carrying a bowl of soup.*]

SARAH BIRD NORTHRUP: Cook burned a whole batch and I had to wait for her to make the next. I hate to make you wait.

JOHN RIDGE: When you're gone, I have nothing to look forward to.

ELIAS BOUDINOT: I'll be leaving now.

SARAH BIRD NORTHRUP: My apologies—

JOHN RIDGE: Don't apologize. Elias was on his way out.

[ELIAS BOUDINOT *exits.* SARAH BIRD NORTHRUP *places the soup on the table next to* JOHN's *bed.*]

JOHN RIDGE: My day consists of three parts: before you bring me soup, when you bring me soup, after you've brought me soup.

SARAH BIRD NORTHRUP: Call me when you finish. Mother hates to find you with dirty dishes.

JOHN RIDGE: Wait for me to finish and you can take them with you.

SARAH BIRD NORTHRUP: I have to sweep the kitchen.

JOHN RIDGE: Arise, fair sun, and kill the envious moon—

SARAH BIRD NORTHRUP: John—

JOHN RIDGE: Who is already sick and pale with grief—

SARAH BIRD NORTHRUP: I have chores.

JOHN RIDGE: It is my lady; O, it is my love!

SARAH BIRD NORTHRUP: We never finished *Macbeth*.

JOHN RIDGE: Look at me, rushing on to *Romeo and Juliet* . . . Let's finish *Macbeth*.

SARAH BIRD NORTHRUP: Not now.

JOHN RIDGE: Twenty pages.

SARAH BIRD NORTHRUP: Mother would notice.

JOHN RIDGE: So what if she did?

SARAH BIRD NORTHRUP: I've been instructed *not* to read Shakespeare with you.

JOHN RIDGE: What's wrong with Shakespeare?

SARAH BIRD NORTHRUP: It's not Shakespeare that concerns her.

[*Beat.*]

I almost forgot. You have a letter.

[*She hands it to him. He continues to look at her.*]

SARAH BIRD NORTHRUP: Are you going to open it?

JOHN RIDGE: Oh. Yes. [*Opening the letter*] It's from my father.

SARAH BIRD NORTHRUP: What does he say? [*Realizing what she has requested*] I'm sorry, how rude of me—

JOHN RIDGE [*reading from the letter*]: He leaves this month for Washington, for meetings at the White House.

SARAH BIRD NORTHRUP: With the president?

JOHN RIDGE: Our leaders routinely meet with the president of the United States, the king of England— [*Continues to read*] He has a position for me! He's speaker of our Tribal Council, and he wants me to assist him!

SARAH BIRD NORTHRUP: You're going home.

JOHN RIDGE: You thought I would stay.

SARAH BIRD NORTHRUP: How foolish of me—

JOHN RIDGE: We have three months. Three months together, from now until I graduate.

SARAH BIRD NORTHRUP: Mother asked me if I loved you.

JOHN RIDGE: What did you say?

SARAH BIRD NORTHRUP: I love the way you take your napkin and wipe the soup bowl dry, I think because you don't want me to spill soup on myself when I climb back down the stairs with your dishes. I love the little poems you write and drop on the floor—

you miss the trash can from your bed, but when you're asleep
I pick them up and read them. I've read all of them. I love your
words, your tenacity, your devotion—

JOHN RIDGE: Marry me.

[Beat.]

SARAH BIRD NORTHRUP: I would if I could.

JOHN RIDGE: I'll talk to your father.

SARAH BIRD NORTHRUP: I already have.

JOHN RIDGE: What did he say?

WOMAN'S VOICE FROM OFFSTAGE [calling]: SARAH!

SARAH BIRD NORTHRUP: The schoolmaster's daughter is not permitted
to marry a savage.

WOMAN'S VOICE FROM OFFSTAGE [calling]: SARAH!

[SARAH BIRD NORTHRUP separates herself from JOHN RIDGE and walks
to the door.]

SARAH BIRD NORTHRUP: I have to go.

WOMAN'S VOICE FROM OFFSTAGE: SARAH!

SARAH BIRD NORTHRUP: I love you, John Ridge.

[She exits.]

SCENE 5

[*1820s. Back at the Cherokee Nation,* MAJOR RIDGE *sits in his home in Rome, Georgia. An envelope lies on the table before him. He studies it. After a few moments,* JOHN ROSS *enters.*]

JOHN ROSS: Major Ridge, sir.

[MAJOR RIDGE *turns to see* JOHN ROSS.]

JOHN ROSS: Two more.

MAJOR RIDGE: When?

JOHN ROSS: Just last night.

[*Beat.*]

Governor Forsyth's instructed—he's actually ordered the militia to violate our women. Any woman who does not obey their command—

MAJOR RIDGE: On Cherokee lands?

JOHN ROSS: They say this is Georgia.

MAJOR RIDGE: We'll go to Washington. Get this all straightened out—

JOHN ROSS: We need to do something more.

MAJOR RIDGE: What do you suggest?

[JOHN ROSS *places a draft bill on the table* and MAJOR RIDGE *regards the piece of paper before him.*]

You drafted this?

JOHN ROSS: It's a rough sketch.

MAJOR RIDGE [*reading*]: "That any citizen of Georgia—" The law is targeted to citizens of Georgia?

JOHN ROSS: We need to make clear the law applies to everyone, Cherokees, non-Cherokees, citizens of Georgia, any non-Indian—

MAJOR RIDGE: How about "person or persons"?

JOHN ROSS: We need to include the Georgia Guard—

MAJOR RIDGE: You think they're excluded from "persons"?

JOHN ROSS: No, no I guess not.

MAJOR RIDGE: They may act like animals, but they're still "persons."

[*Beat.*]

JOHN ROSS [*making the edit*]: "That any person or persons—"

[MAJOR RIDGE *keeps reading.*]

MAJOR RIDGE: "Whatsoever, who shall lay violent hands upon any female, by . . . abusing her person and committing a rape upon such female, . . . shall be punished."

JOHN ROSS: We will prosecute anyone who rapes a woman on Cherokee lands.

[MAJOR RIDGE *nods.*]

I told Chief Hicks we'd have a draft for his review first thing in the morning. Council's set to vote tomorrow.

MAJOR RIDGE: We have the votes?

JOHN ROSS: Two councilmen have said they'll vote against it.

MAJOR RIDGE: From which community?

JOHN ROSS: Guess.

MAJOR RIDGE: I'll speak to them.

JOHN ROSS: This will easily pass. We don't need their votes.

MAJOR RIDGE: Unanimously. On this, we can't be divided. Our women are the foundation of our sovereignty. Without them, we have no nation.

JOHN ROSS: Let me manage your campaign. For chief.

MAJOR RIDGE: My campaign?

JOHN ROSS: Hicks announced he won't run again; everyone's talking about you. I apologize for being so forward, but I've thought a lot about this. I know I'm inexperienced. I'm young. But I can write your speeches. Draft your platform. You've seen my writing—

MAJOR RIDGE: I think *you* should run.

JOHN ROSS: Me?

MAJOR RIDGE: I'll help you write *your* speeches.

JOHN ROSS: No one's done more for Cherokee Nation than you.

MAJOR RIDGE: Everything I've done, we've done together.

[*Beat.* JOHN ROSS *picks up a letter from the table.*]

JOHN ROSS: John wrote you?

MAJOR RIDGE: In English.

JOHN ROSS: You must be awfully proud of him.

MAJOR RIDGE: He graduates in June.

JOHN ROSS: And then he'll move home?

MAJOR RIDGE: I hope so. I asked him to help me, as my special
    assistant.

JOHN ROSS [*reading*]: Hello, Father, spring has finally come and
    already the roses have stretched their thorns—

MAJOR RIDGE: Skip the pleasantries. What does he say?

JOHN ROSS: Yes. He says yes.

MAJOR RIDGE: Splendid.

JOHN ROSS: I look forward to working with him.

MAJOR RIDGE: I want you to mentor him.

JOHN ROSS: Of course.

MAJOR RIDGE: What else does he say?

[JOHN ROSS *reads.*]

JOHN ROSS: Hmm.

MAJOR RIDGE: Well?

JOHN ROSS: I'm not sure—

MAJOR RIDGE: Is it illegible?

JOHN ROSS: No, it's quite legible.

MAJOR RIDGE: Tell me what he wrote.

JOHN ROSS: He wants to marry the schoolmaster's daughter.

MAJOR RIDGE: From Connecticut?

JOHN ROSS: He's asked for your permission.

MAJOR RIDGE: She's *uneg*.

JOHN ROSS: More and more of our men are marrying white women.

MAJOR RIDGE: You married a Cherokee woman, from a good family.

JOHN ROSS: I decided a long time ago that my children would never have to choose the identity of one parent over the other.

MAJOR RIDGE: My grandchildren would have no clan.

JOHN ROSS: He says he's in love.

[*Beat. Then, reading the letter out loud*] "Her father will allow me to marry her if I regain the ability to walk without crutches."

MAJOR RIDGE: That, I fear, will never come to pass.

JOHN ROSS: But if it did?

SCENE 6

[*The present. The Ridge Polson Cemetery, in front of John Ridge's grave.*]

SARAH: This is my great-great-great-grandfather, John Ridge. His dad, Major Ridge, is right next to him. My grandmother, she's just three rows down. Auntie Po, Uncle Buck, my whole family's buried here.

BEN [*from offstage*]: There is just nowhere to pee.

SARAH: Major Ridge, John Ridge, they both signed the treaty—

BEN [*entering*]: How far back is that gas station?

SARAH: Are you listening to me?

BEN: We were in the car for an hour and a half. I have to pee.

SARAH: John's cousin, Stand Watie, over here. John's other cousin, he signed the treaty too.

BEN: The treaty, the treaty, the treaty—yes, I know, all you talk about is the treaty.

SARAH: We don't have to do this.

BEN: Oh, no. I'm happy to be here, I want to be here.

SARAH: You asked me to bring you here—

BEN: I have to pee.

[FLORA *enters.*]

FLORA: Did someone die?

SARAH: Hi Flora.

FLORA: Folks usually only visit when someone's died. But you both look very much alive.

BEN [*to* FLORA]: Hi, I'm Ben.

SARAH: Oh my gosh, I'm so sorry. Flora, this is my boyfriend, Ben.

BEN: Nice to meet you.

FLORA: Will you be buried here?

BEN: I, uh, I'm not sure.

FLORA: I usually only meet my relations' significant others when they decide they'll be buried here.

SARAH: We haven't gotten that far yet.

BEN: Do you have a bathroom?

FLORA: Why?

BEN: I need to pee.

FLORA: That's what trees are for.

BEN: I didn't want to be rude—

FLORA: It's not rude. The cows do it all the time.

BEN: I'll be right back.

[BEN *trots off.*]

FLORA: Sure is nice to see you. I don't hardly see anyone anymore. Unless someone dies. I see lots of folks when someone dies. But then once the funeral's over, everyone goes home. And they don't come back. And then it's just me. And the cows. Who ran over the fence. Had to fix the damn thing myself last year. Replaced it with an electric. It's expensive to keep a cemetery up.

SARAH: I'll make a donation.

FLORA: That'd be nice. I'll put some flowers by your mom.

[*Beat.*]

How's the job?

SARAH: Good. Busy. It keeps me really busy.

FLORA: You like working for a Ross?

SARAH: He's a very smart attorney. I'm learning a lot.

FLORA: You told him who you are?

SARAH: Not yet.

FLORA: Not yet?

SARAH: I'm waiting for, you know, the right time.

BEN [*from offstage*]: AHHHHHHH!!!!! YOUR FENCE IS ELECTRIC!

FLORA: I told him to pee on a tree.

SARAH: Ben?!

FLORA: He'll be fine.

SARAH: Are you OK?

FLORA: I'll get him a towel.

[FLORA *exits.* BEN *enters, with a painful limp in his gait. He attempts, and fails, to hide the pain.*]

BEN: I'm fine—

SARAH: Let's go home.

BEN: No.

SARAH: No?

BEN: Where's your aunt?

SARAH: She went to get you a towel.

[BEN *walks over to* JOHN RIDGE's *grave.*]

BEN: Tell me about your grandfather.

SARAH: Don't you think we should—

BEN [*reading the headstone*]: "Assassinated here June 22, 1839." He was killed here?

SARAH: In his front yard. Just about 150 yards that way. Are you sure you're OK?

BEN: I'm really glad you brought me here.

SARAH: When you're shocked in the penis, does it affect the brain?

[BEN *gets down on one knee in front of* SARAH. *He pulls a small box out of his pocket, opens it up, and presents a ring to* SARAH.]

BEN: Marry me, Sarah.

[*Beat.*]

SARAH: Are you—are you serious?

BEN: You said this was your favorite place.

SARAH: It is. I guess I just—I never expected—

BEN: I wanted to ask you in front of your family.

[*Beat.*]

Sarah Polson—

SARAH: Sarah Ridge Polson.

BEN: Sarah Ridge Polson, will you marry me?

SARAH: Yes.

SCENE 7

[*1828, at the White House.* MAJOR RIDGE, JOHN RIDGE, *and* JOHN ROSS *stand in the foyer of the Oval Office.* JOHN RIDGE *relies on a crutch to walk.*]

JOHN RIDGE [*to* MAJOR RIDGE *and* JOHN ROSS]: I've prepared all of your papers for the meeting with the president.

JOHN ROSS: We need to prioritize the discussion of Georgia's escalating use of violence against Cherokee citizens.

MAJOR RIDGE: Of course.

JOHN ROSS [*to* JOHN RIDGE]: I want you to focus on the Constitution—

MAJOR RIDGE: I'll focus on the courts.

JOHN ROSS: And the circulation of our paper—

MAJOR RIDGE: I agree.

JOHN ROSS: It's critical that we emphasize our sovereignty, and that we're exercising it.

JOHN RIDGE: You think President Jackson will listen?

MAJOR RIDGE: He has to. We're allies, friends from the battlefield.

[ANDREW JACKSON *enters*.]

ANDREW JACKSON: Well, look at this, the Major. Here, in Washington. Have you come to see me?

[MAJOR RIDGE *shakes* ANDREW JACKSON's *hand*.]

MAJOR RIDGE [*in Cherokee*]: *Osiyo*, General.

ANDREW JACKSON: I love this man. [*to* JOHN ROSS] I really, truly love this man.

JOHN ROSS [*nodding*]: President Jackson.

ANDREW JACKSON: Sounds good, doesn't it? And—don't tell me—this must be . . .

JOHN ROSS: John Ross. I serve as the principal chief of the Cherokee Nation.

ANDREW JACKSON: Nothing but the official delegation for me, eh?

JOHN RIDGE: John Ridge. I serve as the assistant to my father, the speaker of our Cherokee Nation Tribal Council.

ANDREW JACKSON: Are you injured?

JOHN RIDGE: I'm recovering, from a long illness.

JOHN ROSS: The doctors said he would never walk. And now he is.

ANDREW JACKSON: With a crutch.

MAJOR RIDGE: *Do-yu o-tsa-li-he-li-ga o-tsa-dv-gi-sgv tsa-da-tlo-sv na da-na-da-sv-ye-sgv-i. (We are so pleased to hear you won the election.)*

JOHN RIDGE: We are so pleased to hear you won the election.

ANDREW JACKSON: I can't thank you enough for your support.

JOHN RIDGE: We were happy to give it.

ANDREW JACKSON: You're well spoken, my boy. A real charm. Just like your father here, your leader, your chief, Major Ridge. He has a way with words. Poetic, really. A real orator, that's for sure. I used to watch him at night, after supper. Men would gather around at all hours of night, until the early morning, just to hear him speak. Couldn't understand a damn word he said, but they listened just the same. Woulda lost at Horseshoe Bend if it weren't for this man and all the Cherokee who followed him into battle. He crossed the Tallapoosa and led the attack from the rear. He won that battle for us, our nation, the entire United States. That's why I named him Major. You know I gave him his name?

JOHN ROSS: The state of Georgia lays claim to our lands, and the federal agents in our midst have begun to play foul.

ANDREW JACKSON: You fear you will lose your land?

JOHN ROSS: The state of Georgia is attempting to take it from us.

JOHN RIDGE: Unlawfully. With violence and fraud.

ANDREW JACKSON: I understand several Tribes are negotiating treaties to sell their lands and move west.

MAJOR RIDGE: *Tla i-lv-hi-yu yi-da-yo-tsa-ni-gis-si ga-do do-gi-hv-i. (We will never leave our lands.)*

JOHN RIDGE: We will never leave our lands.

ANDREW JACKSON: The Choctaw just signed a treaty. They're moving west.

JOHN ROSS: We're not the Choctaw.

ANDREW JACKSON: And the Chickasaw.

JOHN RIDGE: We're Cherokee Nation. And we are not moving.

[GOVERNOR FORSYTH *enters.*]

JOHN ROSS: Governor Forsyth.

[GOVERNOR FORSYTH *waves his copy of the* Cherokee Phoenix *at the* Cherokee *men.*]

GOVERNOR FORSYTH: There's no "e" in Forsyth. F-o-r-s-y-t-h. No "e." Now you got the "e" in governor. It is true there is an "e" there. And there is also an "e" in Georgia. But there's no "e" in Forsyth. I'm sure this is all very confusing for you.

ANDREW JACKSON: If you'll excuse me, gentlemen, I'm scheduled to meet with the governor.

JOHN ROSS: We came all this way to meet with you—

ANDREW JACKSON: And you'll just have to come back some other time.

MAJOR RIDGE: *O-li-i yi-nu-lis-ta-na hna-yu u-na-ye-his-di ge-sv-i tla e-lis-di i-gv-ge-wis-di yi-gi. (Friendship formed in danger should not be forgotten.)*

[ANDREW JACKSON *looks to* JOHN RIDGE.]

ANDREW JACKSON: What did he say?

JOHN RIDGE: Friendship formed in danger should not be forgotten.

[*Beat.*]

ANDREW JACKSON: I say this as your friend. You find yourselves established in the midst of a superior race, and although you do not appreciate the cause of your inferiority, if you do not yield to the force and progress of civilization and move west, you will disappear.

[ANDREW JACKSON *escorts* GOVERNOR FORSYTH *into the Oval Office.* JOHN RIDGE, MAJOR RIDGE, *and* JOHN ROSS *exit.* GOVERNOR FORSYTH *hands* ANDREW JACKSON *the paper.*]

GOVERNOR FORSYTH: Thought you might want to see this.

[ANDREW JACKSON *reads the paper and realizes what it is.*]

ANDREW JACKSON: The Cherokee have a paper?

GOVERNOR FORSYTH: That they circulate from Atlanta to Boston. They wrote a Constitution. They established a court. They think their jurisdiction extends to *United States* citizens living on Cherokee lands.

ANDREW JACKSON: I've always said, take their lands and you'll take their jurisdiction.

GOVERNOR FORSYTH: About that—with all due respect, Mr. President, we have an Indian problem.

ANDREW JACKSON: You and every other governor east of the Mississippi.

GOVERNOR FORSYTH: The Cherokee are an impediment to the expansion of slavery, and cotton, and—

ANDREW JACKSON: The Cherokee have slavery. They own slaves.

GOVERNOR FORSYTH: Their idea of slavery is a farce.

ANDREW JACKSON: They're good people. I assure you, they're not to be blamed for their inferiority.

GOVERNOR FORSYTH: We discovered gold. On Cherokee lands, and the only way we can—

ANDREW JACKSON: Copper, gold, silver, furs, salt, tobacco, sugarcane— all of our industries want to expand but can't because of the Indians. This isn't about Georgia and the Cherokee, or Mississippi and the Choctaw, or Florida and the Seminole. This is about the economy of the entire United States. From the Potawatomi to the Cherokee, until we've moved them all, the progress of the entire nation will be blocked. So be patient. You're not alone. [*Looking at the paper*] Who's this Samuel Worcester?

GOVERNOR FORSYTH: The Reverend. He's a missionary, from Vermont.

ANDREW JACKSON: What's he doing in Cherokee Nation?

GOVERNOR FORSYTH: He brought them the printing press, and he's working with a young Cherokee man by the name of Elias Boudinot to print this paper weekly. In Cherokee and English. And might I add, the federal government pays his salary.

ANDREW JACKSON: To work on a Cherokee paper?

GOVERNOR FORSYTH: To run the postal office. But he spends most of his time working on the paper. Apparently, he's learned to speak Cherokee.

ANDREW JACKSON: I will see to it that he's removed from his position. But you have got to remove him from Cherokee Nation.

GOVERNOR FORSYTH: We have no authority to remove anyone from Cherokee lands—

ANDREW JACKSON: Then make some. Pass a law. Forbid him to be there.

GOVERNOR FORSYTH: With all due respect, Mr. President: Cherokee removal was a campaign promise.

ANDREW JACKSON: Build a fire under them. When it gets hot enough, they'll move.

[GOVERNOR FORSYTH *exits.*]

SCENE 8

[*Back in the Cherokee Nation.* JOHN RIDGE, ELIAS BOUDINOT, *and* SAMUEL WORCESTER *sit at a table prepared for dinner.* JOHN RIDGE *no longer relies on crutches and walks freely about.* SARAH BIRD NORTHRUP *sits next to* JOHN RIDGE.]

SAMUEL WORCESTER: You think we should pull "Recipes for Ensuring Health."

ELIAS BOUDINOT: No. "Sunset in the Alps."

SAMUEL WORCESTER: "Sunset in the Alps" stays. "Recipes" can go.

ELIAS BOUDINOT: Have you ever seen a sunset in the Alps?

SAMUEL WORCESTER: I've never left the United States.

ELIAS BOUDINOT: So why are we covering something none of us have seen?

SAMUEL WORCESTER: We need to seem worldly. Folks in the northeast will know the *Phoenix* is a world-class paper if we discuss the fantastic sunsets in the Alps.

JOHN RIDGE: How about an article on stickball?

SAMUEL WORCESTER: I advise against that.

JOHN RIDGE: Because you think stickball is a sin?

SAMUEL WORCESTER: Those were the words I used in my sermon, yes.

JOHN RIDGE: We've played stickball for thousands of years. When we come together to play, it isn't just a game. It's spiritual.

SAMUEL WORCESTER: It's heathen. And no good Christian man should have anything to do with it.

[MAJOR RIDGE *and* JOHN ROSS *enter.*]

MAJOR RIDGE: My apologies for being late.

JOHN RIDGE: Think nothing of it.

ELIAS BOUDINOT: We just sat down.

JOHN ROSS: I hope we didn't keep you waiting.

JOHN RIDGE: Not at all.

SARAH BIRD NORTHRUP: I'll fix you both a plate.

JOHN ROSS: Thank you.

ELIAS BOUDINOT: Uncle, let me introduce you to the Reverend Samuel Worcester.

[SAMUEL WORCESTER *stands to shake* MAJOR RIDGE's *hand.*]

SAMUEL WORCESTER: So pleased to make your acquaintance.

ELIAS BOUDINOT: And John Ross—

JOHN RIDGE: The chief of our nation.

JOHN ROSS [*extends his hand to* SAMUEL WORCESTER]: It's an honor to finally meet you in person, Reverend.

MAJOR RIDGE: Sarah, our finest silver, please, for our guest.

SARAH BIRD NORTHRUP: Yes.

[SARAH BIRD NORTHRUP *retrieves the finest silver for the Reverend.*]

MAJOR RIDGE: Nothing but the best for the man who brought us the printing press.

SAMUEL WORCESTER: I'm so thankful it's a success.

MAJOR RIDGE: You've caused quite the upset. The president, Governor Forsyth—they're not happy.

ELIAS BOUDINOT: They know about the paper?

JOHN ROSS: Forsyth practically slapped me with it. This paper threatens their entire plan for our removal.

WORCESTER: How so?

JOHN ROSS: The Governors of Georgia, Tennessee, Mississippi, they all say we're uncivilized, uneducated, an obstacle to progress and democracy. They claim *that* is why we must be removed. Imagine their horror when they realized more Americans are reading the Cherokee Phoenix than all of their propaganda combined.

ELIAS: Do you think they'll try to shut us down?

JOHN ROSS: They already are.

JOHN RIDGE: You heard about the law Georgia just passed.

SAMUEL WORCESTER: We're printing an article on it right now.

MAJOR RIDGE: What new law?

JOHN RIDGE: Georgia has made it a crime for any American citizen to set foot on Cherokee lands without their governor's permission.

MAJOR RIDGE: He can't do that.

ELIAS BOUDINOT: I think he just did.

MAJOR RIDGE: We have to challenge this.

JOHN ROSS: Yes, I agree we do.

SAMUEL WORCESTER: According to this law, any American citizen residing on Cherokee lands must sign his allegiance to Governor Forsyth.

MAJOR RIDGE: Well, Reverend.

ELIAS BOUDINOT: He refused.

JOHN ROSS: You refused to sign?

SAMUEL WORCESTER: I sit before you on Cherokee lands in defiance of Georgia law.

JOHN RIDGE: It really *isn't* in defiance of Georgia law because Georgia's laws have no application here. They have no jurisdiction—

ELIAS BOUDINOT: Always the attorney. We'll be sure to state that in our article.

MAJOR RIDGE: We're so thankful that you didn't sign your allegiance. To the governor.

SAMUEL WORCESTER: My allegiance is to the Lord above, and the Lord alone.

JOHN RIDGE: And Cherokee Nation. You're living on Cherokee lands.

[*Beat.*]

SAMUEL WORCESTER: I must say, it's wondrous to arrive in Cherokee Nation and see a friendly face from up north. Sarah, I knew your father.

SARAH BIRD NORTHRUP: Through the church?

SAMUEL WORCESTER: The Board of Missionaries. I helped start the school, in Cornwall, before I moved south. Your father is a true— one of the few remaining true Christian men. The fact that he permitted your marriage—

JOHN RIDGE: He wasn't going to.

SAMUEL WORCESTER: But he did.

JOHN RIDGE: Sarah left him no choice.

SAMUEL WORCESTER: It was entirely his choice—

SARAH BIRD NORTHRUP: He sent me away, to keep me from John. Dropped me off to live at my grandmother's. So I stopped eating. I refused to eat. I almost starved to death.

JOHN RIDGE: Then, and only then, did her father permit our marriage.

SARAH BIRD NORTHRUP: And even then it was contingent on John's ability to walk again. Without crutches.

SAMUEL WORCESTER: He was concerned you were sick.

JOHN RIDGE: He was concerned I was an Indian.

ELIAS BOUDINOT: Reverend, would you like some more corn?

SAMUEL WORCESTER [to SARAH]: Sarah, I think the fact that your father blessed your marriage shows the true merits of his Christian constitution—

SARAH BIRD NORTHRUP: We were attacked. By a mob. Men and women. Dozens of them. As soon as John arrived. The men threw rocks. The women screamed. "Savage. Heathen. You will rot in hell." Those are the words I remember most. My father tried to sneak us out back, but they caught wind of our escape and almost toppled the carriage.

JOHN RIDGE: Any Indian marrying a white girl from Connecticut had better carry a knife.

[*A loud knock at the door.* GEORGIA GUARD *enters, armed with a gun.*]

GEORGIA GUARD: Reverend Worcester?

SAMUEL WORCESTER: That's me.

GEORGIA GUARD: You're under arrest.

ELIAS BOUDINOT: For what?

GEORGIA GUARD: Violating the law.

JOHN RIDGE: That you passed yesterday?

GEORGIA GUARD: Georgia's law.

JOHN RIDGE: Georgia's laws have no application here.

JOHN ROSS: This is Cherokee Nation.

GEORGIA GUARD: This man entered Cherokee lands without the permission of the governor—

SARAH BIRD NORTHRUP: He's here to preach the gospel.

GEORGIA GUARD [*turns to* SARAH]: Do you live here?

SARAH BIRD NORTHRUP: I do.

GEORGIA GUARD: With the permission of the governor?

JOHN ROSS: With the permission of Cherokee Nation.

GEORGIA GUARD: It is illegal for any white man, or woman, to set foot on Cherokee soil without the permission of the governor of Georgia.

MAJOR RIDGE: She's married to a Cherokee.

[*He leans in.*]

GEORGIA GUARD: Does that make you *Cherokee*?

54

JOHN RIDGE: She's my wife.

GEORGIA GUARD: Your wife? [*To* SARAH] You know, we've been instructed to violate Cherokee women who do not obey our commands.

MAJOR RIDGE: Leave her alone.

SAMUEL WORCESTER [*steps forward*]: You came to arrest me. Please.

[GEORGIA GUARD *escorts* SAMUEL WORCESTER *off.*]

SCENE 9

[*Georgia, 1832.* SAMUEL WORCESTER *sits in jail. Five days have passed since his arrest.* JOHN RIDGE *enters.*]

SAMUEL WORCESTER: How's my wife?

JOHN RIDGE: Good.

SAMUEL WORCESTER: My children?

JOHN RIDGE: They're great. Really great.

SAMUEL WORCESTER: Are they scared?

JOHN RIDGE: Elias is taking good care of them.

SAMUEL WORCESTER: Tell them I will see them on Monday.

JOHN RIDGE: Monday?

SAMUEL WORCESTER: I told the governor I'm going to sign his paper.

JOHN RIDGE: You can't do that—

SAMUEL WORCESTER: I let them arrest me, I made my statement, and now I've spent five days in jail.

JOHN RIDGE: I'm only asking for a few more.

SAMUEL WORCESTER: To do what?

JOHN RIDGE: Challenge your conviction. In the Supreme Court—

SAMUEL WORCESTER: That could take years.

JOHN RIDGE: Or maybe months. Depending on how fast—

SAMUEL WORCESTER: I want to go home. I miss my family. I can't stay here—

JOHN RIDGE: This isn't about you.

SAMUEL WORCESTER: I seem to be the one sitting here.

[*Beat.*]

It's nothing more than a piece of paper. And when I sign it, I get to go home.

JOHN RIDGE: What does it say?

SAMUEL WORCESTER: That I entered Cherokee lands without Georgia's permission.

JOHN RIDGE: Georgia has no jurisdiction on our lands.

SAMUEL WORCESTER: They have soldiers. And they're arresting people like me, anyone who does not obey their command—

JOHN RIDGE: They arrested you to make a statement. If they can enter our lands and remove you, they can remove me. And every other citizen of the Cherokee Nation.

SAMUEL WORCESTER: I think it's inevitable—

JOHN RIDGE: They want to establish a precedent. And you're willing to give it to them.

SAMUEL WORCESTER: I want to go home.

JOHN RIDGE: So you'll let them take mine.

[*Beat.*]

SAMUEL WORCESTER: Perhaps we should pray. Or I could read to you. From the Bible. In Cherokee. That's all I have done since I've been here. My translations. [*Picks up some pages and hands them to* JOHN] Tell Elias I stopped at John chapter 7, verse 24. "Judge not according to the appearance, but judge righteous judgment." Now, "judgment" in Cherokee, that's hard to translate.

You do not read the Bible.

JOHN RIDGE: My faith is in the Cherokee Constitution. Not the Bible.

SAMUEL WORCESTER: The two aren't mutually exclusive.

JOHN RIDGE: Then why is one being used to extinguish the other?

SAMUEL WORCESTER: I left everything I've ever known to help you, to help Elias translate the entire Bible into Cherokee. When I sign the governor's paper, I get to return to that work. But an appeal to the Supreme Court would . . . it would prevent me from finishing the work I came here to do—

[GEORGIA GUARD *enters.*]

GEORGIA GUARD: Five minutes. [*To* JOHN RIDGE, *very slowly, over-enunciating*] Fiiiiivvveee minnnnuttttesssss.

[GEORGIA GUARD *points to the ornate watch on* JOHN RIDGE's *wrist and flashes all five fingers. To* SAMUEL WORCESTER]

Tell your friend here he's got five minutes, then he's gotta go.

JOHN RIDGE: I can tell time. I can also speak English.

GEORGIA GUARD: Well now, that's a first.

JOHN RIDGE: Did you know that, at this very moment, Cherokee Nation citizens can read and write at rates higher than the citizens of Georgia?

GEORGIA GUARD: Do you defy me? [*To* SAMUEL WORCESTER] I think he defies me.

JOHN RIDGE: Defy an officer of the state of Georgia? Who's ever heard of such a thing?

GEORGIA GUARD: I oughta arrest you right now.

SAMUEL WORCESTER: Please, officer, we were about to pray.

GEORGIA GUARD: Oh. Well now. I gotta hear that. Never heard an Indian pray before. Let me hear you pray, boy. Let me hear you pray for that heathen soul. I SAID, LET ME HEAR YOU PRAY.

SAMUEL WORCESTER: He believes in Christ, officer. I've heard him profess his faith numerous times.

GEORGIA GUARD: There's a special place in hell for savages like you.

[GEORGIA GUARD *exits. Beat.*]

SAMUEL WORCESTER: If you were to appeal my conviction, what would you argue?

JOHN RIDGE: Georgia had no authority to arrest you on Cherokee lands because Cherokee Nation is the *only* sovereign with jurisdiction over Cherokee lands. John Ross and I prepared the papers, and we've secured the assistance of William Wirt, former attorney general under Adams.

SAMUEL WORCESTER: What do you need from me?

JOHN RIDGE: Your signature.

SAMUEL WORCESTER: Just tell me where to sign.

SCENE 10

[*The present. Friday night. Sarah's house.* ROGER, SARAH, BEN, FLORA, *and* WATIE *sit around the kitchen table. The table is full of food.*]

BEN: So would you say that Indians—I mean Native Americans—

FLORA: You can call us Indians.

ROGER: But we prefer "Injun."

BEN: Sure.

SARAH: Dad.

BEN: I didn't know, you know, until I met Sarah, that Injuns believe in—

SARAH: *Indians*. Don't listen to him.

BEN [*nods*]: I didn't know y'all were Christians.

ROGER: Some of us even drive cars. Government's got this program now. Trade your pony in for a car. Indians only though. Just one of the perks, the *benefits*, that come with being Indian.

SARAH: He's joking.

BEN: Oh, ha.

ROGER: You know why the Cherokee hate snow?

BEN: Uh, it's cold and wet, and pretty miserable.

ROGER: It's white and covers all of our land.

WATIE: He's really proud of that one.

SARAH: Can you pass the potatoes?

FLORA: Ketchup?

[FLORA *passes her the ketchup.* SARAH *shakes the ketchup but nothing comes out.*]

SARAH: You know why the Cherokee love ketchup? It's red and no matter how hard you shake it, it refuses to move. It's permanently stuck.

BEN [*laughs awkwardly*]: That's a good one.

ROGER: How'd you propose to my daughter?

BEN: Well, you know, I asked her—I said, what's your favorite place on earth? And she told me the cemetery where her grandfathers are buried—

ROGER: The cemetery?

BEN: Yeah, where your folks are buried—

ROGER: You proposed to my daughter in the cemetery?

FLORA: It was romantic.

SARAH: It was perfect.

FLORA: Until he peed on my fence.

ROGER: Who proposes in a cemetery?

SARAH: He wanted to ask me in front of our family.

ROGER: I'm sitting right here. And I don't recall anyone asking me anything.

BEN: I hadn't met you yet, sir—

ROGER: You're meeting me now.

SARAH: Daddy.

ROGER: You gonna have kids?

[SARAH *and* BEN *look at one another.*]

SARAH: I think so, yes.

BEN: Yeah.

ROGER [*to* BEN]: They'll be Cherokee Nation citizens?

BEN [*looks around for help*]: Can they? I don't have any Indian blood.

ROGER: You don't need Cherokee blood to be Cherokee. Just ask the freedmen.

SARAH: Dad.

BEN: Freedmen?

FLORA: Descendants of slaves. That the Cherokee owned.

BEN: Y'all owned slaves?

SARAH: We did.

WATIE: The majority of Cherokee didn't.

FLORA: But we did.

BEN: We aren't the only ones!

FLORA: They just won their court case.

WATIE: We signed a treaty with the United States, after the Civil War—

SARAH: And in that treaty, we agreed to grant citizenship to all former Cherokee slaves.

WATIE: Twenty years ago we amended our Constitution and disenrolled all of them.

SARAH: One of the most embarrassing moments of our history.

ROGER: They're not Cherokee.

SARAH: They walked the Trail of Tears.

ROGER: Is that what makes you Cherokee? Walking the Trail of Tears?

SARAH: Sovereignty isn't about race. It's about citizenship. And they're citizens. We signed a treaty!

BEN: And we know how you feel about treaties.

ROGER [to BEN]: What do *you* know about treaties?

BEN: I know your folks signed one. And then they were killed.

FLORA: By the Rosses.

SARAH: John Ross had nothing to do with the assassinations.

FLORA: His party killed more than one hundred and fifty members of the Ridge treaty party—

SARAH: Members of his political party carried the murders out and he was only informed after—

FLORA: He knew. He knew that as soon as they made it to Oklahoma—

SARAH: Indian Territory. Oklahoma wasn't a state yet.

FLORA: He knew as soon as they got to *Indian Territory*, they planned to show up at John Ridge's house, drag him out of his bed—

SARAH: I think it's a bit more complicated than that—

ROGER: Ross was a dictator.

FLORA: He canceled the elections.

ROGER: He shut down the paper.

FLORA: He ruled like a tyrant.

ROGER: And yet Cherokees walk around today worshipping him.

FLORA [*to* BEN]: And Rosses say that we, the Ridges, caused the Trail of Tears.

ROGER [*to* BEN]: When Cherokee Nation moved west, the nation was paid five million dollars. You know where that money went? From the United States directly to Ross's brother. And that's how Lewis Ross became the first millionaire in Cherokee Nation. Everyone blames the Ridges for the Trail of Tears, but the Rosses profited from it. They made millions.

BEN [*to* SARAH]: Ross? That's who you work for, that's your boss?

[SARAH *nods yes.*]

ROGER: You work for a Ross?

SARAH: Jim Ross. In the attorney general's office.

ROGER: You never told me.

SARAH: You never asked.

WATIE: I've met him. He's a nice guy.

ROGER: I can't believe you're working for a Ross.

SARAH: Well I am.

FLORA: If it were me, I'd shoot him.

SARAH: Please don't say that.

ROGER: It's about time someone killed a Ross in Tahlequah.

SARAH [to ROGER]: Back to your question—our kids will be Cherokee because I'm Cherokee.

FLORA: Cherokees are matrilineal.

BEN: So kids follow the mother?

ROGER: You haven't even discussed this.

SARAH: We haven't gotten that far but—

ROGER: You have no idea if he'll agree to enroll your children as Cherokee Nation citizens?

SARAH: You don't give a shit about being Cherokee.

ROGER: I'm proud of who I am.

SARAH: Your idea of being Cherokee is sleeping under a Pendleton blanket and drinking out of a Cherokee Nation coffee mug.

WATIE: Sarah.

SARAH: He left. He left and he never came back. He never brought us back. We had to come back. On our own. Without him.

ROGER: I'm here now.

SARAH: Because I called you. Because I begged you, Daddy, please come back to Oklahoma. Please, Daddy, come back and walk me down the aisle.

ROGER: I wouldn't walk you down the frozen pizza aisle to meet this guy.

[ROGER *exits.*]

WATIE: Just because you finally decided to come home doesn't mean he has to.

[WATIE *exits, after his father.*]

SARAH: Ugh. The men in my family.

BEN: He'll change his mind.

FLORA: He's never changed his mind about anything.

SARAH: Seriously. What's his problem?

FLORA: You were disrespectful.

SARAH: Me? What about him?!

FLORA: He's sensitive. He's been through a lot.

SARAH: He's an asshole.

FLORA: True. But he's also your father.

SCENE 11

[*1832. Cherokee Nation. Major Ridge's home.* JOHN RIDGE, MAJOR RIDGE, JOHN ROSS, *and* ELIAS BOUDINOT *meet with the attorney, former United States attorney general* WILLIAM WIRT.]

WILLIAM WIRT: How is the Reverend?

JOHN RIDGE: In good spirits. They have him making cabinets.

JOHN ROSS: I thought he was sentenced to hard labor.

MAJOR RIDGE: *Di-se-his-di dv-go-tlv-sgv do-yu sda-ya, nas-gi-na-i yo-ne-ga yi-gi. (Making cabinets is hard, for a white man.)*

[JOHN RIDGE, ELIAS BOUDINOT, *and* JOHN ROSS *laugh.*]

WILLIAM WIRT: I beg your pardon?

ELIAS BOUDINOT: Making cabinets is hard, for a white man.

JOHN RIDGE: My father means no offense.

JOHN ROSS: It's just our sense of humor.

WILLIAM WIRT: He understands English.

MAJOR RIDGE: Yes.

WILLIAM WIRT: But he can't speak it?

MAJOR RIDGE: *Do-yu u-go-da go-hv-sdi tsu-da-le-nv-da yi-ni-tsi-wi Tsa-la-gi gv-di na-no tla yi-ni-ge-tsi-wi Gi-li-si gv-di. Ga-da-yi-ha e-sga ya-wa-da-dv-di-i. (There are so many things I can say in Cherokee that I cannot say in English. I refuse to limit myself.)*

JOHN RIDGE: There are so many things he can say in Cherokee that he can't say in English. He refuses to limit himself.

JOHN ROSS [*to* WILLIAM WIRT]: You plan to focus your argument on our treaties?

WILLIAM WIRT: They're very strong documents.

JOHN RIDGE: You have a list of all the treaties we've signed?

WILLIAM WIRT: Got it right here.

ELIAS BOUDINOT: I think you start with Hopewell.

JOHN RIDGE: That treaty recognizes Cherokee Nation's sovereign right to exercise jurisdiction over all Cherokee lands.

WILLIAM WIRT: I plan to review it tonight.

JOHN RIDGE: And your Constitution makes clear that once a treaty is signed by your president and ratified by your Senate, it becomes the supreme law of the land.

ELIAS BOUDINOT: So the law is on our side. They have no law.

WILLIAM WIRT: They have an audience. This president, and the justices he appointed, they're all very sympathetic to the state.

JOHN RIDGE: But what about the law? The court's decision must be based on the law, not sympathies.

WILLIAM WIRT: I must be honest with you. There's hardly a politician in Washington that isn't advocating for your removal. Did you know the state of Georgia has attempted to have my license to the bar revoked? For representing you. They have allies in Washington, and you do not.

MAJOR RIDGE: *Hi-a u-na-da-la-su-lv tla ga-nvs-bi-da ge-sv-i yu-ye-li-da yi-gi. Tla yu-dv-di u-hv-i na-sgi u-li-tsa-di o-sda ka-no-he-da u-ye-li-da yi-gi na-hna-i. Tsa-la-gi ga-do u-ni-hv-i tsu-ga-ti-lv-da na sga-du-gi a-ga-ti-ya u-du-lis-gv-gi. Hi-a du-na-da-la-su-lv nv-ye-li-dv na-sgi yi-ga-dv-ne-li-da-sdi i-gi-hv di-ga-se-sdo-di di-ga-tse-li a-ne-hi-ya u-na-i i-ga-tse-li ga-do-i. Hi-a i-gi-hv i-ga-da-tse-li-ga-ya na-sgi nu-ye-li-da. (This case isn't about a missionary. It isn't about his right to preach the gospel on Cherokee lands against the governor's wishes. This case is about our right to protect our citizens on our land. It's about our sovereignty.)*

[WILLIAM WIRT *looks to* JOHN RIDGE.]

JOHN RIDGE: This case isn't about a missionary. It isn't about his right to preach the gospel on Cherokee lands against the governor's wishes. This case is about our right to protect our citizens on our land. It's about our sovereignty.

WILLIAM WIRT: All the same, I need to state something a bit more . . . concrete. In the brief. I'll cite to your treaties—

JOHN ROSS [*points to Major Ridge*]: When he was born, the United States didn't exist. After winning the war, the first thing General Washington did was sign a treaty with the Delaware Lenape. You see, fifty years ago, the whole world recognized the sovereignty of Indian Nations, but no one recognized the United States.

JOHN RIDGE: They used our sovereignty to establish the United States, and now they seek to destroy it.

WILLIAM WIRT: What is *sovereignty*?

JOHN ROSS: What is it to you?

WILLIAM WIRT: My good friend Webster, in his dictionary, defines "sovereignty" as "a country's independent authority and the right to govern itself." And I have cited that, in the brief I've begun to write—

JOHN ROSS: When we established our Supreme Court, that's sovereignty.

ELIAS BOUDINOT: When the council votes on a resolution, that's sovereignty.

JOHN RIDGE: *Na-yu-no ya-gi-wo-ni-si a-gi-wo-ni-hi-sdi na-sgi-na-i u-nv-sa u-ni-hv di-gu-go-ta-ni-da-sdi ge-so-i. (Sovereignty is when I speak my language.)*

[WILLIAM WIRT *looks to* JOHN ROSS *for the translation.*]

JOHN ROSS: Sovereignty is when I speak my language.

WILLIAM WIRT: That's . . . provocative. I'm just not sure how to work it into the brief—

[JOHN RIDGE *hands him a drafted brief.*]

JOHN RIDGE: Don't worry, I've drafted it for you.

WILLIAM WIRT: Oh.

JOHN RIDGE: The brief starts with an analysis of article two, section two, clause two of your Constitution—

JOHN ROSS: John's an attorney.

WILLIAM WIRT [*to* JOHN RIDGE]: You practice law?

JOHN RIDGE: I studied it. But no court in the United States will allow me to practice it on account of my race.

JOHN ROSS: We can sign documents to sell our lands, but we can't speak on our own behalf when we ask your courts to enforce the agreements your nation has signed with us.

WILLIAM WIRT [*to* JOHN RIDGE]: Thank you. I'm grateful for your help.

JOHN RIDGE: But you feel forced to accept it.

WILLIAM WIRT: You must forgive me. I didn't expect you to have prepared arguments based on *our* Constitution.

JOHN RIDGE: It's a very straightforward document.

JOHN ROSS: John, Elias, the Major, all of us are at your disposal. We'll help you in any way we can.

WILLIAM WIRT: Very well then.

JOHN ROSS: It's late.

WILLIAM WIRT: Yes and the trip was long—

JOHN RIDGE: We will resume tomorrow.

WILLIAM WIRT: Thank you.

MAJOR RIDGE: *Do-ya-di-dla yi-wi-gv-ya-ka-hv-ga. (I will escort you out.)*

ELIAS BOUDINOT: The Major will escort you.

WILLIAM WIRT: Goodnight, gentlemen.

[MAJOR RIDGE *escorts* WILLIAM WIRT *off.*]

JOHN ROSS [*to* JOHN RIDGE]: I used to translate. For your father. Until you both came back from Cornwall. And then . . .

JOHN RIDGE: Your Cherokee is quite good.

JOHN ROSS: I didn't speak until I was ten. And even then, I only spoke in phrases.

JOHN RIDGE: I learned English when I was twelve.

JOHN ROSS: Your English is excellent.

JOHN RIDGE: I've learned a lot from listening to you.

JOHN ROSS: I wanted to speak our language. When I was a boy. But every time I tried, my father scolded me. Speaking Cherokee was "uncivilized." So I spoke English. Until I met your father.
My father married a Cherokee woman, but somehow he never expected a Cherokee son. Goodnight.

[JOHN ROSS *exits.*]

ELIAS BOUDINOT: You submitted a powerful brief.

JOHN RIDGE: We took your edits.

ELIAS BOUDINOT: I saw that.

JOHN RIDGE: You have the uncanny ability to take cluttered sentences and reorganize them in the most compelling fashion.

ELIAS BOUDINOT: I just removed a few words here and there. You're too verbose. But that's why you have me. Even the most brilliant mind needs an editor.

[SARAH BIRD NORTHRUP *enters.*]

JOHN RIDGE: Goodnight, Elias.

[ELIAS BOUDINOT *nods and exits.*]

SARAH BIRD NORTHRUP: I pressed your suit. The one your father bought you for graduation. I fixed the tear in the seam from your last trip to Washington. And please, John, watch what you put in your pockets. Pockets are for small items. Like handkerchiefs. Or combs. A key or two.

JOHN RIDGE: Notes from your wife?

SARAH BIRD NORTHRUP: Notes from your wife, yes. But not rocks. You can't put rocks in your pocket, no matter how interesting they look when you find them in your path.

JOHN RIDGE: What if I want to bring one home to you?

SARAH BIRD NORTHRUP: You're the most brilliant man I've ever met, but when it comes to common sense, Creator did not bless you.

JOHN RIDGE: You know that in the history of the United States, no Indian Nation has ever won a case in your Supreme Court. Ever.

SARAH BIRD NORTHRUP: Maybe you'll be the first.

SCENE 12

[*The present.* JIM ROSS *sits in his office in the Cherokee Nation (Oklahoma).* SARAH *joins him.*]

SARAH: Jury acquitted.

JIM ROSS: Oh, no.

SARAH: Defense impeached my key witness, my other witness recanted, and the defendant came across as really reliable, trustworthy—the jury loved him.

JIM ROSS: I know you're disappointed.

SARAH: They're so good at that. The abusers we prosecute. Watie shows up at the scene, she's bloody and bruised, he's screaming, blood on his hands, and then you put her on the stand and she goes silent, and you put him up there and the jury loves him.

JIM ROSS: Hey, [*pointing to her ring*] when are you gonna tell me about this ring you've been flashing around? Congratulations.

SARAH: Oh, thank you.

JIM ROSS: Who's the lucky man?

SARAH: Ben. O'Connor.

JIM ROSS: Sarah O'Connor.

SARAH: He's a cop. For the state.

JIM ROSS: Too bad your name isn't Sandra Day.

[*Beat.*]

OK, so we have to go back to D.C. Tomorrow.

SARAH: To meet with the DOJ?

JIM ROSS: The president.

SARAH: Like, of the United States?

JIM ROSS: He has some questions about the legitimacy of tribal jurisdiction—

SARAH: Questions?

JIM ROSS: You may not be surprised to hear that this president isn't as supportive of tribal jurisdiction as the one you watched sign it into law in 2013.

SARAH: He wants to take away the jurisdiction Congress restored?

JIM ROSS: He's considering it.

SARAH: Congress passed VAWA. And he's the president—he can't just defy Congress. If he wants to change VAWA—

JIM ROSS: Let's not debate the constitutionality of what he wants, or thinks he can do. Let's just help him understand jurisdiction. We'll have ten minutes with the president. I'm looking to you to tell me what to say.

SCENE 13

[*1832. Oval Office.* JOHN RIDGE *enters and speaks to* ANDREW JACKSON.]

JOHN RIDGE: If I'm correct, this is the first time an Indian Nation's ever won in your Supreme Court.

[*Beat.*]

I'm sure by now you've read Justice Marshall's decision.

[*Beat. He reads from the copy of the decision he holds in his hand.*]

"The Cherokee Nation then is a distinct community, occupying its own territory, with boundaries accurately described, in which the laws of Georgia can have no force"—this is what Justice Marshall has declared. Georgia has no jurisdiction over Cherokee lands.

[ANDREW JACKSON *continues to stare at him.* JOHN RIDGE *decides to continue.*]

As I'm sure you are aware, Georgia has refused to release Reverend Worcester. They continue to force him to undertake hard labor, despite the court's decision compelling his release. Even worse, Georgia has begun to survey our land. They've created a lottery, and they're giving away Cherokee lands to Georgia citizens, in violation of Cherokee law.

[Beat.]

How do you plan to enforce the Supreme Court's decision? Georgia refuses to comply, and they won't, not without federal intervention.

[Beat.]

I've read your Constitution. I understand its meaning. As the president, you are constitutionally required to enforce the law of this land, and the Supreme Court has declared the law.

ANDREW JACKSON: John Marshall made his decision. Let him enforce it.

ACT 2

SCENE 1

[SARAH *joins* BEN *in their living room. Photos of cakes surround* SARAH *and* BEN. SARAH *sits with her laptop open.* BEN *holds a sheet of paper with a form to fill out.*]

BEN: You OK?

SARAH: I feel nauseous.

BEN: You're anxious. You need to calm down.

SARAH: This is important. I can't make a mistake. What do you think of this sentence? "VAWA's restoration of Cherokee Nation's criminal jurisdiction is an important step to the full restoration of the jurisdiction preserved in the Treaty of New Echota." That's a reference to the treaty my grandfathers signed.

BEN: So Jim will delete it.

SARAH: Probably. Ugh.

BEN: Hey.

[BEN *holds out the cake options in front of her laptop.*]

Pick one.

SARAH: Oh. I don't know.

BEN: Chocolate or vanilla.

SARAH: Both.

BEN: Not an option.

SARAH: That's ridiculous.

BEN: You can have both, just not in the same cake.

SARAH: OK, so two cakes.

BEN: We budgeted for one.

SARAH: You choose. I can't right now.

BEN: I got a call from the florist.

SARAH: Oh shit.

BEN: You still haven't put in the order for the flowers.

SARAH: What'd we decide? Yellow and turquoise?

BEN: You said you would choose.

SARAH: I think it was purple and turquoise—

BEN: And you said you would place the order three months ago.

SARAH: I'm really sorry. Oh, and I can't meet with the caterer tomorrow, so you'll have to go alone.

BEN: Why?

SARAH: I have to go to D.C.

BEN: Again?

SARAH: I just found out today—

BEN: To do what?

SARAH: We're meeting with the president.

BEN: Who is "we"?

SARAH: What is this, twenty questions?

BEN: It will be if you refuse to give me an answer.

SARAH: I gave you an answer.

BEN: Who's going to D.C?

SARAH: Me. And Jim.

BEN: I'll come too.

SARAH: It's not really that kind of a trip. We'll be working the whole time.

BEN: I can entertain myself. I won't bother you.

SARAH: I'll be gone and back in less than thirty-six hours.

BEN: I don't understand why you don't want me to come.

SARAH: I don't understand why you're making this such a big deal.

BEN: Because Jim's a jerk. He attacks your family constantly, and you hate him. I don't want you alone in D.C with him. I worry about you. On your own with him.

SARAH: I'll die before I let a Ross intimidate me.

BEN: I've been SVU for ten years, and sometimes—I can't explain it, I get this feeling. And with Jim, all I can say is, I don't trust him.

SARAH: But you trust *me*.

BEN: Tell him you can't go.

SARAH: We already got the plane tickets.

BEN: Tell him you're getting married.

SARAH: This is my job.

BEN: And I'm your fiancé.

SARAH: I can't believe you would ask me to stay.

BEN: I'm not asking.

SCENE 2

[*Two nights later. On the night Sarah is to return from D.C.* MITCH *and* BEN *sit at the casino bar, drinking beers.*]

BEN: She wants to push it back.

MITCH: When'd she say that?

BEN: Right before she left. Kissed me on the cheek and then said, "I'm having second thoughts about April. How about September?" and she was out the door. September?

MITCH: People change their dates all the time.

BEN: I'm worried she changed her mind.

[BEN *raises his hand for the* BARTENDER, *who serves* MITCH *and* BEN *another beer. They continue to drink.*]

MITCH: Only one way to find out.

BEN: Soooo, Sarah, seems like you don't want to marry me anymore?

MITCH: I wouldn't phrase it like that.

BEN: You're the lawyer. Tell me how to interrogate the witness.

MITCH: You're the cop. You know it's all about the evidence. You have to catch her in the moment. You know, when she's said or done something that undeniably shows she's questioning the marriage.

BEN: I'm such a fool.

MITCH: Everyone goes through this.

BEN: What made me think she was in love?

MITCH: What did she say when you popped the question?

BEN: She said yes. You think I'm forcing her to marry me?

MITCH: Did she say, "Oh my god, yes!" Or "Sure, why not"? There's a difference. And did she have to think about it?

BEN: Jesus, Mitch, she said "Yes."

[BEN *notices a text on his phone.*]

She just landed.

MITCH: Be strong. Tell her the wedding date can't be pushed back and see how she responds. If she's not fully in, you wanna know now. Because when you get to the other side, it ain't pretty.

BEN: We haven't even married yet and you're already talking divorce.

MITCH: I do it for a living.

[BEN *flags down the* BARTENDER.]

BEN: One for the road.

[*He looks at his phone again*]

What the fuck.

MITCH: What?

BEN: She's getting a ride with Jim.

MITCH: Her boss?

BEN: "Don't need you to pick me up. Getting ride with Jim." [*To the bartender*] Hey, make that a Maker's Mark. On the rocks.

[BARTENDER *nods and attends to the drink.*]

MITCH: Hey man—

BEN: Every day Jim reminds Sarah that most of Cherokee Nation thinks her grandfathers are traitors because of some treaty they signed. And then she comes home and cries to me. And I comfort her—I tell her, it's OK, babe, Jim's a jerk. Be strong. You can do it. He's an asshole. And what does she do? She decides to postpone our wedding so she can go off to D.C with Jim, the jerk.

[BEN *inhales his drink.*]

MITCH: Hey man, pace yourself.

BEN: Is this something Indian women do?

MITCH: I'm sorry?

BEN: Do they run around—you know—like this?

MITCH: I'm not sure what you mean.

BEN: You kissed one. Did she turn around and kiss every other kid on the playground?

MITCH: I kissed Sarah.

BEN: What?

MITCH: I kissed Sarah, and then I don't think she kissed anyone else in our class for years. I think I ruined it for her. She probably never wanted to kiss anyone until she kissed you.

BEN: You never told me you kissed my fiancée.

MITCH: She wasn't your fiancée when I kissed her. OK. That was fifth grade. We were kids.

BEN: So that's the only time you've kissed my fiancée?

MITCH: You need to calm down.

BEN: You need to stop kissing my fiancée and hiding it from me!

[BEN *grabs his coat and he's off.*]

MITCH: I don't think you should—BEN!

[BEN *is gone.* MITCH *exits.*]

SCENE 3

[*Moments later.* SARAH *and* JIM ROSS *open the door to Sarah and Ben's home. They step inside,* JIM *carries her suitcase.*]

SARAH: Ben?

[*She walks a bit farther.*]

SARAH: Ben? [*To* JIM ROSS] Guess he's not here. Come on in.

JIM ROSS: Are you sure?

SARAH: It's raining.

JIM ROSS: I don't want to intrude.

SARAH: Ben won't care. I don't know where he is.

JIM ROSS: Did I hear you tell the president your grandfathers were treaty signers?

SARAH: Oh, yeah. I wanted him to understand the connection, that when I go to D.C, I follow in their footsteps.

JIM ROSS: Which treaty did they sign?

SARAH: I didn't realize how late it is.

JIM ROSS: Hopewell?

SARAH: We did circle the airport twice. Did you see the lightning in that storm?

JIM ROSS: Are you descended from Hicks?

SARAH: I'll get us some water.

JIM ROSS: OK, come on. Who were your grandfathers?

[BEN *enters his home.*]

BEN: Jim.

JIM ROSS: Ben.

SARAH: I was wondering where you were.

BEN: I didn't expect to come home and find him standing in my kitchen.

SARAH: I invited him in.

JIM ROSS: I gave her a ride home.

BEN: Does that require you to enter my home?

SARAH: It's raining.

BEN: I noticed.

JIM ROSS: I'm gonna go ahead and leave now.

BEN: You sure you don't want to stay? You know, kiss my fiancée?

SARAH: Are you drunk?

JIM ROSS: See you tomorrow.

SARAH: I'll be there.

BEN: Me too!

SARAH: Ben?

BEN: Oh, I'm not invited.

JIM ROSS: Goodnight.

BEN: Get the fuck out of my house.

[JIM ROSS *exits.*]

SARAH: What is wrong with you?

BEN: What's wrong with *you*?

SARAH: Are you drunk?

BEN: Did you enjoy your trip?

SARAH: I have news. Exciting news. That I really want to tell you.

BEN: Yes, please, tell me, how was your time with *Jim*?

SARAH: I'm serious, Ben—

BEN: Did you have fun?

SARAH: I'm pregnant.

[*Beat.*]

> I missed my period, by a lot, and remember how I was so nauseous this past week? I went to a CVS in D.C and got one of those kits, the test, and it came back positive.

[*Beat.*]

I know it's not what we planned—I know we wanted to be married first, but we both said we want to be parents, so . . . we are! We're going to have a baby!

BEN: You slept with Jim.

SARAH: What? No.

[BEN *slaps her across the face.*]

BEN: I'm your fiancé, Sarah.

[*She steps back from him.*]

SARAH: You need to leave.

BEN: So you can be with Jim?

SARAH: You need to leave because you just hit me.

BEN: Sarah, that's not what I—

[BEN *presses his body against hers, pushing her up against the wall.*]

SARAH: You're hurting me.

[SARAH *tries to escape his hold.*]

BEN: Say you're sorry.

SARAH: Ben—

BEN: SAY YOU'RE SORRY.

[SARAH *spits in his face. He punches her squarely in the face, and she falls to the ground. He unzips his pants.*]

SCENE 4

[*Cherokee Nation, 1832.* JOHN ROSS *sits with* ELIAS BOUDINOT *and* MAJOR RIDGE *in his home.* JOHN RIDGE *enters.*]

JOHN RIDGE: He says he won't enforce it.

[*Beat.*]

ELIAS BOUDINOT: What do you mean?

JOHN RIDGE: He won't enforce the Supreme Court's decision.

ELIAS BOUDINOT: But he has to.

JOHN RIDGE: And I'm telling you he won't.

JOHN ROSS: He's their president.

JOHN RIDGE: He laughed at me.

MAJOR RIDGE: The Supreme Court is their highest court.

ELIAS BOUDINOT: Did you visit our friends in Congress?

JOHN RIDGE: I met with Justices Marshall and McLean, our friends in Congress. I visited everyone we know in Washington.

JOHN ROSS: Congress will make him follow the court.

JOHN RIDGE: No one will defy the president. They all say we should sign a treaty and move west.

JOHN ROSS: No. Never. Tell them we say never.

[*Beat.*]

JOHN RIDGE: I think we have no choice.

JOHN ROSS: We just won the right to remain on our lands and you think we should move?

JOHN RIDGE: What good is a right that will never be enforced?

JOHN ROSS: So we wait. For the next president.

JOHN RIDGE: That could be years.

JOHN ROSS: Or months. Jackson could lose his reelection.

JOHN RIDGE: He's going to win. Americans love him—

JOHN ROSS: We will never leave.

JOHN RIDGE: Every day, more and more are killed by the Georgia Guard.

JOHN ROSS: Our land is who we are. It's what makes us Cherokee.

JOHN RIDGE: What use will our land be once we've all been killed?

ELIAS BOUDINOT: He has a point—Georgia's outlawed our government, they rape our women, half our nation is now homeless—

JOHN ROSS: And so we should give up, let go, give it all away?

JOHN RIDGE: I do not say this lightly. I see no other way for our nation to survive. If we agree to move west, we'll lose our lands, but we'll preserve the nation. Intact.

[*Beat.*]

JOHN ROSS [*to* JOHN RIDGE]: I drafted the blood law. With your father. Anyone who sells Cherokee lands to the United States will be prosecuted and sentenced to death.

JOHN RIDGE: Things have changed.

JOHN ROSS [*to* JOHN RIDGE]: The only thing that's changed is you. Your father and I agreed. We promised each other. We will never leave. We will never sign a removal treaty. We will always stay.

JOHN RIDGE: If we stay, we will only perish.

JOHN ROSS [*to* JOHN RIDGE]: There are consequences to what you say.

JOHN RIDGE: I'm prepared to accept them.

JOHN ROSS [*to* MAJOR RIDGE]: He's turned against us. He's forsaken everything we stand for.

[*Beat.*]

Tell him he's wrong. Remind him what we agreed to. Years ago. You and I.

[*Beat.*]

JOHN ROSS: As principal chief of Cherokee Nation, it is my job—no, it is my *duty*—to protect my people against those who seek to separate us from our lands.

[SARAH RIDGE POLSON *enters and approaches* JOHN ROSS.]

SARAH RIDGE POLSON [*to* JOHN ROSS]: Sorry I'm late.

JOHN ROSS [*softens*]: It's fine—

SARAH RIDGE POLSON: I know we have a training.

SCENE 5

[*The present, the next day. Attorney general's office, Cherokee Nation.* JIM ROSS *and* SARAH *speak in the attorney general's office.*]

JIM ROSS: We've got four new prosecutors coming on board, and I was hoping you could speak to them. Two are fresh out of law school, but the two senior prosecutors are coming to us from the state. Should have a pretty good team here . . . Look, I know you're a rock star, but when you're in the office, maybe you can remove the shades. Don't want you to intimidate the new hires. They're kinda shy.

[JIM ROSS *takes off* SARAH'*s sunglasses. Her eye is surrounded by a purple and blue bruise.*]

[*With incredible concern*] He did this?

[*She nods.*]

Are you safe?

[*She nods ambivalently.*]

You have a place to stay?

SARAH: I have family.

JIM ROSS: Why don't you take some time off. You should—

SARAH: No.

JIM ROSS: Where'd he do this?

SARAH: My home.

JIM ROSS: That's ... that's Cherokee Nation.

[*She nods.*]

We have jurisdiction.

[*She takes the shades back and puts them on.*]

SARAH: I want Cherokee Nation to prosecute.

SCENE 6

[*1832. New Echota, Cherokee Nation.* ELIAS BOUDINOT *and* JOHN RIDGE *sit at the* Cherokee Phoenix *office, paper stretched out before them.*]

ELIAS BOUDINOT: "John will be our next chief, says the talking leaf."

JOHN RIDGE: Which John?

ELIAS BOUDINOT: Good point. Uh, "In a time of crisis, we will need a bridge. Vote for John Ridge."

JOHN RIDGE: "Sovereignty First. John Ridge for chief."

ELIAS BOUDINOT: That doesn't rhyme.

JOHN RIDGE: Does it need to?

ELIAS BOUDINOT: It's not a slogan unless it rhymes. Such as, "He may look like a goat, but John Ridge deserves your vote."

JOHN RIDGE: "Don't give John Ross your vote, he'll turn around and shove it down your throat."

ELIAS BOUDINOT: A bit aggressive.

JOHN RIDGE: I'm not convinced it has to rhyme. So long as it's clear I'm the Treaty Party candidate.

ELIAS BOUDINOT: You've said nothing of John Walker.

JOHN RIDGE: I was with him last night.

ELIAS BOUDINOT: When he was shot?

JOHN RIDGE: Before James Foreman shot him. On his way home. From council.

ELIAS BOUDINOT: The Ross Party wants to murder you. And me. And every member of the Treaty Party.

JOHN RIDGE: This is one killing.

ELIAS BOUDINOT: They're sending a message! Anyone who advocates for removal will be killed.

JOHN RIDGE: We're more likely to be killed by a citizen of Georgia than one of Ross's crew.

ELIAS BOUDINOT: Maybe we should slow down—

JOHN RIDGE: Slow down?

ELIAS BOUDINOT: Take a step back—

JOHN RIDGE: And watch Georgia take our homes? Rape our women? Murder our families?

ELIAS BOUDINOT: You need to think about how you campaign. That's all I'm saying. Not change your position—just think about how you communicate it. People are scared. They're terrified. They know we need to talk about it. But when you come out and say that if elected, the first thing you'll do is sign a treaty, people get defensive, they—

[JOHN ROSS *enters.*]

ELIAS BOUDINOT: Morning, chief.

JOHN ROSS: John, Elias, I want you to know elections have been canceled.

JOHN RIDGE: You can't do that.

JOHN ROSS: We're experiencing a constitutional crisis.

ELIAS BOUDINOT: The Constitution calls for an election. Every four years.

JOHN ROSS [*to* ELIAS BOUDINOT]: Tell me, Elias, why are you printing articles advocating for Indian removal?

JOHN RIDGE: There are elected leaders of the Cherokee Nation who believe removal is the best course of action to preserve the nation.

JOHN ROSS: Those leaders constitute a small—and I mean very small—minority. They do not speak for the nation.

JOHN RIDGE: That's why you canceled the elections.

JOHN ROSS: We are under attack. From all sides.

ELIAS BOUDINOT: You're opposed to discussing a removal treaty—

JOHN ROSS: *Cherokee Nation* is opposed—

ELIAS BOUDINOT: All the same, sir, I believe the power of a paper is its dissemination of all viewpoints. A paper does not tell people what or how to think.

JOHN ROSS: This paper is circulated across the entire United States.

ELIAS BOUDINOT: A circulation I worked hard to cultivate.

JOHN ROSS: I will not have President Jackson reading anything that says there are Cherokees who favor removal. If you print another article advocating for removal, Council will suspend your funding.

ELIAS BOUDINOT: You would fire me?

JOHN ROSS: Cherokee Nation tax dollars will not be spent securing the nation's demise.

ELIAS BOUDINOT: Then you must accept my resignation.

JOHN ROSS: That is your choice—

ELIAS BOUDINOT: I have come to the unpleasant and most disagreeable conclusion that our lands, or a large part of them, are about to be seized and taken from us. There is danger, immediate and appalling, and so it is my job—no, it is my duty—to act consistently, give alarm, and tell our countrymen our true, or what I believe to be our true, situation.

JOHN ROSS: I accept your resignation.

[Beat.]

JOHN RIDGE: I hear they took your home. I heard that when you got back from your last trip to Washington, you found a white family living in your home.

JOHN ROSS: Georgia "granted" it to them.

JOHN RIDGE: That's why we should sign a treaty—they're taking our homes. But if we agree to move—

JOHN ROSS: We will never move.

JOHN RIDGE: Your wife and children were living in your storeroom. And paying rent. Just to live in the storeroom.

JOHN ROSS: Who are *you* to talk to me about family?

JOHN RIDGE: My father thought of you as his son.

JOHN ROSS: Tell your father that advocating for the sale of Cherokee lands is a crime punishable by death.

SCENE 7

[*Present day. Tahlequah, Oklahoma.* ROGER *sits at Sarah's kitchen table, reading the* Cherokee Phoenix.]

ROGER [*calls*]: Is he asleep?

[*He returns to his paper.*]

 [*Louder*] Hey! Is he asleep?

[SARAH *enters, dressed for work. And late. She carries* BABY RIDGE.]

SARAH: Yes, and don't yell. You'll wake him!

ROGER: Sorry.

SARAH: He was up at four thirty. Wouldn't go back to sleep until now.

ROGER: So he's cranky.

SARAH: He's a baby.

ROGER: You wrote everything down?

SARAH: It's all right here.

[*She points to a pad of paper on the table.*]

I'm taking my breast pump with me.

ROGER [*hands over his ears*]: I don't need to hear about you pumping your breasts.

SARAH: I'm a mother. It's what mothers do.

ROGER: And I'm your father. Please don't talk to me about it.

SARAH: There are three bottles in the fridge. That should get you through the day. You have my phone number—

ROGER: We'll be fine.

[SARAH *hands* BABY RIDGE *to* ROGER.]

SARAH: My lunch break's at noon and—

ROGER: Go on now. You can't be late your first day back.

[SARAH *goes to exit. She stops.*]

SARAH: Dad, thank you.

[SARAH *exits.*]

ROGER [*holds* BABY RIDGE, *asleep in his arms*]: OK, first things first. When you wake up, Mom's not gonna be here. And that, well, it might feel like a surprise. And you'll be like, who is this guy? He smells like cashews. And Lucky Strikes. But don't tell your mom I smoke. She thinks I stopped.

I'm your grandpa. You're my first grandkid. So, you know, I've never done this before. But I raised your mom. And your uncle. They think they had it rough. But me, shit, I was ten when I went to Chilocco. I know the slap you get for speaking your language, and I know the laugh when someone's laughing at you 'cause of who you are.

Your mom named you Ridge. Ridge, *John* Ridge, was my mom's great-grandfather. That's something to be proud of—he was a brilliant man, a fighter. His blood runs through your veins. Never forget that. Just don't tell anyone you're named after him. It's, like, between you and me. Our little secret.

The day they find out you're a Ridge is the day they kill you.

SCENE 8

[MITCH *and* BEN *sit at the bar in the Hard Rock Casino, Catoosa, Oklahoma.* BARTENDER *is present, but neither* BEN *nor* MITCH *ever request (or need) a refill.*]

MITCH: They've dismissed you from the force.

BEN: I have ten years of excellent service.

MITCH: And now you have a domestic violence conviction.

BEN: In a tribal court. You and I both know that doesn't count. You know who they put on my jury? Seven Indians, two black guys, and two—only two—white people. And they were both women! How is THAT a jury of my peers?

[MITCH *moves* BEN's *beer away from him.*]

MITCH: We need to focus. Next time, we meet in my office.

BEN: It's too far for me to drive—

MITCH: We can't have these conversations in a casino.

BEN: What's wrong with supporting the Cherokee Nation? I'm in their courts, I might as well be in their casino. [*He raises his beer*] To the Cherokee fucking Nation!

MITCH: We lost your habeas challenge.

BEN: In the Tenth Circuit?

MITCH: Decision came out this morning.

BEN: So we appeal to the Supreme Court.

MITCH: That's definitely an option, but—

BEN: Let's go all the way.

MITCH: Supreme Court's not gonna grant cert on a case like this.

BEN: Grant cert?

MITCH: Certiorari. Granting cert, it's lawyer speak for "agree to hear the case"—

BEN: They "granted cert" in Dollar General's case—

MITCH: That resulted in a four–four tie—

BEN: And now there's a ninth justice. Gorsuch and Kavanaugh are gonna vote against tribal jurisdiction.

MITCH: I wouldn't be so sure about that—

BEN: We can pick up where Dollar General left off.

MITCH: You want me to argue that tribal jurisdiction—*any* tribal jurisdiction over American citizens—is unconstitutional.

BEN: Uh, yeah. Because it is. Wait. Do you actually think tribal jurisdiction over me *is* constitutional?

MITCH: I think as an attorney I need to make the best argument possible for my client.

BEN: I'm asking you what you think. As my friend.

MITCH: You've asked me to be your attorney. That's very different. Let's focus on the argument.

BEN: Tribal jurisdiction over non-Indian American citizens violates the Constitution.

MITCH: I'm gonna have to say a bit more than that. I'll start with *Oliphant* and its justification. Explain that, yes, the court did give Congress some discretion in administrating over Indian affairs, but that doesn't permit Congress to recognize a tribe's jurisdiction over non-Indians—

BEN: Because doing so violates the constitutional rights of individual Americans.

MITCH: Sure.

BEN: I mean, you can't tell me these courts are legitimate. Some elder climbs to the top of the mountain, smokes tobacco, comes back down with a decision. Seriously. What's that.

MITCH: You were tried before a jury, not on a mountaintop.

BEN: A jury full of Indians! How do you think they made their decision? I bet you they prayed.

MITCH: You need to let me do my job.

BEN: I'm the one coming up with all of the arguments.

MITCH: Your arguments aren't arguments. I'm an attorney.

BEN: You do family law.

MITCH: Yes, and what I say has to have some basis in the law.

[WATIE *enters, in uniform. He stops when he sees* BEN *and* MITCH.]

BEN: Look who it is.

[WATIE *turns around to leave, but stops when* MITCH *calls to him.*]

MITCH: I've tried calling you. I don't know if, maybe you didn't get my voicemails.

[*Beat.*]

I'd really like to talk. Maybe not here, but maybe sometime we could get together—

WATIE: I have nothing to say to you.

MITCH: Everyone deserves an attorney. In fact, it's a constitutional right we all have that when we're accused of a crime, we get to have an attorney.

WATIE: Did you see the photos? Did you see what he did to her?

MITCH: I did.

WATIE: Ben didn't "mess up." This wasn't an "accident."

MITCH: He had too much to drink. He got angry; things got out of control.

WATIE: He's been sentenced to three years in jail.

BEN: We're appealing to the Supreme Court.

WATIE [*to* BEN]: You will pay for what you did.

BEN: Look, man, I know some awful, like super awful, things have happened to you people over the last five hundred years. The Trail of Tears. I get it. You're angry. But it's 2020. Time to let it go.

WATIE [*to* MITCH]: You're dead to me.

MITCH: He's my friend.

WATIE: And what is my sister?

MITCH: She's my friend too.

WATIE: That's funny. We thought you were family.

[WATIE *exits.*]

MITCH: So back to the discussion of your appeal.

BEN: You work on custody cases.

MITCH: Usually, yes.

BEN: Let's file for custody.

MITCH: I think we need to focus on the case we'll make now, to the Supreme Court—

BEN: Sarah'll drop the charges if we file for custody. We could make a trade. She drops the charges, I drop the custody suit.

MITCH: Honestly, with a DV charge against you—

BEN: From a fake court!

MITCH: Just the same, it's a DV charge, and no judge is going to award you—

BEN: He's MY son. And I have a right to be a father to my son.

MITCH: You said he *wasn't* your son. You told me Jim got her pregnant.

BEN: That baby's mine.

MITCH: So you lied to me.

BEN: Have you looked at that baby? Blond hair. He has my eyes. He's white. No way he's a real Cherokee. He's like, a *fraction* Cherokee.

MITCH: I'm withdrawing my representation of you.

BEN: The fuck, you can't do that!

MITCH: I'll help you find a new attorney. A public defender—

BEN: I should have known not to trust an attorney who's kissed opposing counsel.

MITCH: Sarah's a good person. I can't do this to her.

[MITCH *exits.*]

BEN: Hey man. I'll take one more.

BARTENDER [*to* BEN]: I'm not Cherokee, so you know. What do I know. I just work for the nation. But I serve a lot of guys a lot of booze, guys like you. Guys with money. Guys with no money. They sit at my bar and I make their drinks. And I listen. To what they say. And when they talk about how it's time for the Indians, for the Cherokee who are still here today to just "get over it" and "let it go," I wonder, when are *you* gonna let it go? When will guys like you get over it? Andrew Jackson lost. The Cherokee are still here. And as for me, well, I hope they always will be.

SCENE 9

[SARAH *sits in her office, working.* JIM ROSS *enters.*]

JIM ROSS: The Supreme Court granted cert.

[*Silence.*]

His brief is due in thirty days. We have sixty.

[*More silence.*]

I know this is bad news.

SARAH: He's arguing that the exercise of tribal jurisdiction over non-Indians violates the United States Constitution.

JIM ROSS: His petition cites *Oliphant*. Like twenty-nine times.

SARAH: He didn't know that case existed until I told him.

JIM ROSS: It's a good case for him.

SARAH: He knows how I feel about *Oliphant*!

JIM ROSS: That's why he's using it. Against you. And he got the attorney, the same attorney who represented Dollar General in the Supreme Court—

SARAH: The attorney who argued that no Tribe should be able to exercise jurisdiction over a non-Indian who sexually assaults an Indian child on tribal lands?

JIM ROSS: That's the one. He's a very distinguished Supreme Court litigator—

SARAH: We should drop the charges. Against Ben.

JIM ROSS: You mean, like, let him go?

SARAH: If we drop the charges, if we let him go, his constitutional claims will be moot and there won't be anything for the Supreme Court to decide.

JIM ROSS: We've worked so hard for this—

SARAH: We could lose our jurisdiction. The court could say tribal jurisdiction over non-Indians is unconstitutional.

JIM ROSS: Or the court could say it IS constitutional.

SARAH: Name me one time that's ever happened.

JIM ROSS: *Worcester v. Georgia.*

SARAH: Right. And then almost one hundred and fifty years later, the court decided *Oliphant.*

JIM ROSS: *Worcester* has never been declared bad law. It's still good precedent.

SARAH: To historians, maybe.

JIM ROSS: To me. Look, I know this is personal to you. Deeply personal. But this case is personal to me too. To most Cherokees, *Worcester* is a great case that we won. To me, it's a responsibility.

A duty. An obligation. It's my grandfather's legacy. And nothing, not even *Oliphant*, can erase what Justice Marshall wrote in *Worcester*. My goal is to make the court recognize that.

SARAH: And what if they don't?

[*Beat.*]

JIM ROSS: This is your decision to make. Just think about it.

SCENE 10

[WATIE *and* FLORA *sit on the couch in* SARAH's *apartment watching TV.* ROGER *enters carrying* BABY RIDGE.]

ROGER [*telling the Cherokee creation story to* BABY RIDGE, *in Cherokee*]: *El-o-hi a-gv-yi tsi-ge-sv u-wa-na-de-s-gi, wa-ni-ge-i, a-le ga-du-li-da ge-sv-gi. Na-s-gi-no nv-gi di-ni-nv-sa-di du-ni-ya-we-tsv a-ni-ga-ti-yv-i. (At first the earth was flat, soft, and wet. The animals grew tired of waiting.)*

[ROGER *stops when he sees* WATIE *and* FLORA.]

ROGER: I'm telling him a story.

WATIE: Didn't mean to interrupt.

ROGER [*continuing in English*]: No one even knows how long they had been there, but they were anxious to get down from the sky vault, so they sent different birds out to see if it was dry.

[WATIE *sits on the couch and turns the TV on.* FLORA *leans over* ROGER's *shoulder to speak to* BABY RIDGE.]

FLORA: But there was no place to land so they all came back to Gal-vladi to wait some more. Finally, it seemed the earth might be dry enough, but they still weren't sure—

WATIE: That was a poop.

ROGER: What? No.

WATIE: He pooped.

FLORA: I heard it.

ROGER: He's passing gas.

FLORA: Give it three minutes, you'll smell the shit in that baby's diaper.

ROGER: One 'a you two wanna change it?

WATIE [to FLORA]: You're the babysitter.

FLORA [pointing to WATIE]: You're the uncle.

ROGER: There are responsibilities that come with being an uncle.

WATIE: Changing diapers isn't one of them.

[SARAH enters.]

ROGER: So they sent out the Great Buzzard to go and see if it was ready for them all to come down.

FLORA [to SARAH]: He just woke up.

SARAH: Oh, did you? Baby Ridge, my baby boy. [Smelling his diaper] Oh, geez. You guys didn't smell that?

ROGER: Smell what?

SARAH: He pooped.

ROGER: I guess babies do that.

SARAH: Where's the diaper bag?

FLORA: Kitchen.

ROGER: I'll get it.

[ROGER *exits, taking* BABY RIDGE *with him.*]

WATIE: Hey, so I got a call from Jim today. He says I need to talk to you—

SARAH: I've decided to drop the charges.

FLORA: What?

SARAH: I told Jim we should let Ben go.

FLORA: After what he did to you?

WATIE: Dad!

ROGER [*from offstage*]: What?

WATIE [*to* SARAH]: You can't drop this case.

SARAH: I can if I want to—

WATIE: DAD!

SARAH: This is MY decision—

WATIE: Dad, seriously. Get in here—

[ROGER *returns with a clean* BABY RIDGE.]

ROGER: What's all this screamin' about?

WATIE: Sarah told Jim to release Ben. To drop the charges.

ROGER: Is that true?

SARAH: Yes.

WATIE: She can't do that.

SARAH: I can if I want to—

WATIE: Tell her she has to call Jim right now—

SARAH: Watie!

WATIE: Tell him no way you're ever gonna agree to drop those charges—

SARAH: I've made up my mind.

ROGER: So you're gonna quit.

SARAH: This isn't quitting.

ROGER: You're just pausing?

SARAH: We're dropping the charges. Lawyers do it all the time.

ROGER: Not this lawyer.

[SARAH *takes* BABY RIDGE.]

SARAH: If we lose—if we lose this case in the Supreme Court, Ridge will spend the rest of his life as the son of the attorney who lost the nation's jurisdiction. I can't do that. I can't make my baby an exile in his own nation.

[*Beat.*]

ROGER: I told you, don't go back. If you do, they'll kill you. That's what my mom told me. It's what her dad told her.
    The one time I did go back, I was nineteen, unemployed, and needed a job. I walked into the employment office and handed the woman there my citizenship card. She looked at me with judgment. "Are you still ostracized for what your grandfathers did?" So I said to her, all they ever did was fight to save the nation.

Your nation. My nation. And what did they get in return? My grandfather was stabbed. Forty-eight times in front of his wife and children. She laughed. She laughed. So I left. Walked right out. I never came back. Until you brought me back. I'm here because of you.

So quit the case. Cancel the appeal. Do whatever lawyerly thing you need to do. But I see the difference between you and me. You've never quit anything in your life.

[ROGER *exits*. WATIE *watches his father leave and then follows.*]

[JOHN RIDGE *enters and approaches* FLORA. SARAH RIDGE POLSON *remains.*]

[*Cherokee Nation (Georgia), 1835.*]

JOHN RIDGE: I'm headed over to Elias's house.

SARAH BIRD NOTHRUP: It's going to snow.

JOHN RIDGE: I have my coat.

SARAH BIRD NOTHRUP: Why don't you wait and finish your work tomorrow?

JOHN RIDGE: Reverend Schermerhorn's here.

SARAH BIRD NOTHRUP: John Ross said yes?

JOHN RIDGE: He said no.

SARAH BIRD NOTHRUP: So you're . . .

JOHN RIDGE: Going to sign without him. My father, Elias, Uncle, Ross's son, we have a group of forty or so that have agreed to sign.

[*Beat.*]

SARAH BIRD NOTHRUP: But, the blood law.

[*Beat.*]

JOHN RIDGE: A small price to pay to save the nation.

SARAH BIRD NOTHRUP: Don't sign it.

JOHN RIDGE: I've made up my mind.

SARAH BIRD NOTHRUP: Let your father, let your uncle, let the older men sign this treaty. Don't add your name to theirs.

JOHN RIDGE: What kind of leader advocates for the signing of a removal treaty and then when presented with quill and paper turns the other way?

SARAH BIRD NOTHRUP: A leader that is a husband. And a father. Of five. Five children who love and adore him.

[*Beat.*]

SARAH BIRD NOTHRUP: There must be some other way.

JOHN RIDGE: I wish there was.

SARAH BIRD NOTHRUP: Jackson's term is almost over—

JOHN RIDGE: I've met with every politician in Washington—

SARAH BIRD NOTHRUP: The next president might enforce the Supreme Court's decision—

JOHN RIDGE: Everyone says we should move west. The only allies we have are missionaries. And they don't care where we reside, so long as we read the Bible.

I've spent years trying to convince your nation to enforce a decision from its highest court. The violence has only escalated.

If we stay much longer, we won't have a Cherokee Nation. We'll have a few Cherokee survivors, if we're lucky.

[*Beat.*]

SARAH BIRD NOTHRUP: You have an impossible decision to make. I wish you didn't have to make it. But you do.

When my father told me I couldn't marry a "savage," I told him I'd rather die than live without you. He laughed, and so I asked him to define "savage." You know what he said? Someone who isn't civilized. And I said what's "civilized?" And he said, "someone who lives by the rule of law." And so now I ask, who is more savage? A nation who makes laws and abides by them, or a country who makes laws and refuses to enforce them?

We are both willing to die for what we love.

JOHN RIDGE: Will you forgive me?

SARAH BIRD NOTHRUP: Forgive you?

JOHN RIDGE: For choosing my nation over my family.

SARAH BIRD NOTHRUP [*to* JOHN RIDGE]: Your family is your nation.

[JOHN RIDGE *embraces her.*]

SARAH BIRD NOTHRUP: I love you, John Ridge.

[JOHN RIDGE *exits.*]

SCENE 11

[JIM ROSS *is working at his desk.* SARAH *approaches him.*]

SARAH: Don't drop the charges.

JIM ROSS: Wait, you don't—

SARAH: I changed my mind. I have to fight this. If he can erase my sovereignty over my body, he can erase the sovereignty of my nation.

JIM ROSS: I want you to do the argument.

SARAH: What?

JIM ROSS: In the Supreme Court.

SARAH: I've never argued in the Supreme Court.

JIM ROSS: You have to start sometime.

SARAH: There's a lot riding on this case.

JIM ROSS: And we need someone who understands that.

SARAH: You don't know me.

JIM ROSS: I know you're brilliant—

SARAH: But you don't know who I am.

JIM ROSS: If you don't want to do it, I won't make you.

SARAH: I want to do it.

JIM ROSS: Then what's your problem?

SARAH: I'm a Ridge.

JIM ROSS: Ridge. Like . . .

SARAH: John Ridge.

JIM ROSS: Like John Ridge. Wow.

SARAH: I'm a direct descendant. He is my grandmother's great-grandfather. I should have told you. A long time ago, I know. But then you wouldn't have hired me. Or maybe you would have fired me. And what am I supposed to say? I am who I am. I can't change that.

[Beat.]

Say something. Anything. Please, don't just stand there.

JIM ROSS: John Ridge betrayed our nation. He signed the treaty.

SARAH: To save Cherokee Nation—

JIM ROSS: My grandfather, John Ross, he was the chief of Cherokee Nation. John Ridge wasn't elected—

SARAH: Because Ross canceled the elections. He wouldn't let John Ridge run.

JIM ROSS: I was taught, you know, growing up—

SARAH: To disrespect him.

JIM ROSS: I don't know him.

SARAH: But you judge him.

JIM ROSS: He paid the price. For what he did.

SARAH: You think he deserved it.

JIM ROSS: He signed the treaty.

SARAH: So you hate him.

JIM ROSS: I didn't say I *hate* him—

SARAH: You can't hate him and respect me.

JIM ROSS: I respect you, Sarah—

SARAH: His blood runs through my veins!

[*Beat.*]

JIM ROSS: John Ridge betrayed our nation. You think he saved it. We won't resolve this in a day, or a month or even a year. But we have something now, something just as pressing, if not more pressing, before us. So could we, maybe just this once, leave all that behind us and fight for what both of our grandfathers fought for, and that is the sovereignty of Cherokee Nation? I'm asking you, Sarah Polson—

SARAH: Sarah *Ridge* Polson.

JIM ROSS: Sarah Ridge Polson, will you argue on behalf of the Cherokee Nation in the United States Supreme Court?

SARAH: Yes.

SCENE 12

[ELIAS BOUDINOT's *home. New Echota, Cherokee Nation, December 29, 1835.* SARAH RIDGE POLSON *watches as* JOHN RIDGE *enters and finds* ELIAS BOUDINOT *and* SAMUEL WORCESTER. MAJOR RIDGE *enters with* REVEREND SCHERMERHORN, *who carries and lays out the Treaty of New Echota on the table before them.*]

ELIAS BOUDINOT [*to* JOHN]: We're ready to sign.

[*They study the treaty.*]

MAJOR RIDGE: *Ha-tlv di-ka-hna-wa-dv-sdi na a-hv di-gu-go-ta-ni-da-sdi? (Where is the provision on jurisdiction?)*

JOHN RIDGE: My father won't sign this treaty unless it preserves our exclusive jurisdiction over Cherokee lands—

REVEREND SCHERMERHORN: Article five.

JOHN RIDGE: "The lands ceded to the Cherokee nation in the forgoing article shall, in no future time without their consent, be included within the territorial limits or jurisdiction of any State or Territory"—

ELIAS BOUDINOT: We will maintain exclusive jurisdiction over our lands?

REVEREND SCHERMERHORN: Yes.

MAJOR RIDGE: *Ga-nv-si-dv wi-de-ga-la-wi-gi na-hna e-la-di di-ga-la-wi-sdi wa-tsi-ni a-ye-li-i na-sgi o-gi-no-he-lv-i. (We discussed a representative in Congress.)*

ELIAS BOUDINOT: Our representative in Congress—

REVEREND SCHERMERHORN: Article seven. Cherokee Nation "shall be entitled to a delegate in the House of Representatives of the United States." I promise you, everything we discussed. It's in there.

[ELIAS BOUDINOT *points and* MAJOR RIDGE *nods as they continue to read the treaty.*]

REVEREND SCHERMERHORN [*watching the Cherokee with great anxiety*]: Sure is cold out there. Maybe it'll be warmer where you go. I don't know. Never been there. Government's never sent me that way, they always send me here.

[JOHN RIDGE, MAJOR RIDGE, *and* ELIAS BOUDINOT *reach agreement. They nod and begin, one by one, to sign.*]

REVEREND SCHERMERHORN: Maybe you'll grow corn out there. I got to see your Green Corn dance once when I was down here. I can't say I fully understood it.

[ELIAS BOUDINOT *hands* JOHN RIDGE *the quill.*]

REVEREND SCHERMERHORN: Just waiting for you, John!

[JOHN RIDGE *signs the treaty.*]

REVEREND SCHERMERHORN [*takes up the treaty*]: Feels good to finally get it signed, right? After all these years of negotiations. Must feel good to just be done with it. Weight off your shoulders.

MAJOR RIDGE: *A-wu-sa a-yo-hv-hi-sdi a-da-ni-yv-do-di go-we-lv-ga. (I just signed my death warrant.)*

REVEREND SCHERMERHORN: What did the Major say?

ELIAS BOUDINOT: I just signed my death warrant.

REVEREND SCHERMERHORN: I'll transport this to Washington immediately.

[REVEREND SCHERMERHORN *exits.* MAJOR RIDGE *puts his hand on his son's shoulder.*]

SAMUEL WORCESTER: I wish it hadn't come to this.

ELIAS BOUDINOT: What is a man who will not dare to die for his people?

JOHN RIDGE: Who is there here that will not perish, if this great nation may be saved?

[ELIAS BOUDINOT *sings* "Amazing Grace" *in Cherokee.* SAMUEL WORCESTER *and* MAJOR RIDGE *join him.*]

SCENE 13

[The present. The United States Supreme Court. Oral argument.]

SARAH RIDGE POLSON: Good morning. Sarah Ridge Polson for the Cherokee Nation. May it please the court. One hundred and eighty years ago, my great-great-great-great-grandfather served as speaker of the Cherokee Nation Council that established the Cherokee Nation Supreme Court. We opened our Supreme Court in 1825, twenty years before the state of Georgia opened its own.

At that time, like today, our Cherokee women were raped and assaulted by non-Natives who visited and lived on Cherokee lands. At that time, like today, Cherokee Nation passed a law criminalizing the rape of women on Cherokee lands. And Cherokee Nation prosecuted perpetrators regardless of whether they were Indian or not. If you raped a woman on Cherokee lands, you would be prosecuted by Cherokee Nation.

In 1832, Georgia fought Cherokee Nation's jurisdiction. In response, this court declared Cherokee Nation's jurisdiction to be both exclusive and inherent. In *Worcester v. Georgia*, this court upheld the inherent right of Indian Nations to protect their citizens.

President Jackson, however, refused to enforce the court's decision. Instead, he openly defied it, and in 1837, Jackson stacked this court with justices he felt would abide his mission to erase tribal jurisdiction and, ultimately, Tribal Nations.

Andrew Jackson's policies, unfortunately, lasted long after his life. Jackson's fight to eliminate tribal jurisdiction culminated in 1978, when this court declared that Tribal Nations were no longer able to exercise jurisdiction over non-Indians who commit crimes on tribal lands. Following this court's decision in *Oliphant*, rates of non-Indian violence against Native women on tribal lands skyrocketed, as non-Indian offenders realized tribal governments were now without the authority to prosecute them for their criminal behavior. Today Native women face rates of domestic violence and sexual assault higher than any other population in the United States. It took one hundred and forty years to fully come into effect, but Andrew Jackson's campaign to eliminate tribal jurisdiction has reaped devastating, life-and-death consequences for Native women.

Like the arguments Georgia and President Jackson used to support the forced removal of Cherokee Nation, the petitioner's arguments are based on a prejudicial view that tribal governments, tribal courts, tribal constitutions, and the entirety of tribal law must be inferior to the law created and enforced by the states and the federal government.

But we're not. Nothing about us, or our governments, is inferior. Petitioner's argument that Indian Nations cannot exercise jurisdiction over non-Indians finds no support in the Constitution. Tribal jurisdiction over non-Indians predates the United States Constitution. So tribal jurisdiction isn't unconstitutional. It's preconstitutional.

And no sovereign, not even the United States, can strip my nation of its inherent right to protect me and my fellow Cherokee women. Thank you. *Wado.*

SCENE 14

[*1838.* JOHN RIDGE *arrives at the Hermitage plantation.* ANDREW JACKSON *has two pies on the coffee table before him.*]

ANDREW JACKSON: Can I offer you some pie?

JOHN RIDGE: I'm not hungry.

ANDREW JACKSON: You have to be, traveling so far. How many days since you left Georgia?

JOHN RIDGE: I left *Cherokee Nation* the first of May.

ANDREW JACKSON: Got apple and pumpkin. Take your pick.

JOHN RIDGE: There are thousands who refuse to leave. They've been informed of the treaty, but Ross told them not to leave. He's told the entire nation the treaty is illegitimate and the federal government cannot require them to leave.

ANDREW JACKSON [*helps himself to a piece*]: I prefer apple myself. Never much liked pumpkin.

JOHN RIDGE: I realize you're no longer in the White House, but perhaps you could speak to the current administration and impress upon them that the Cherokee cannot be forced to move at gunpoint. If the United States does that, there will be deaths—

ANDREW JACKSON: This here, this is my wife's recipe. Thank God she taught the help before she passed. I do not know what I would do if I had to continue without her apple pie. Losing her was bad enough. Now, your wife is white, correct?

JOHN RIDGE: She's from Cornwall, Connecticut.

ANDREW JACKSON: So your children are half Cherokee.

JOHN RIDGE: My children are not fractions. They're citizens. Of a sovereign nation. Cherokee Nation.

ANDREW JACKSON: Hmm. Sometimes I have to wonder how many times you can cut an apple pie before it's no longer apple.

[He cuts another piece of apple pie.]

I mean, this, this piece here, this is apple pie.

[He places it in the one empty slot where a piece of pumpkin pie had previously been cut and eaten.]

But when I place it here, what is this? I think most people would say this pie is pumpkin. There is, of course, a piece of apple. Just a tiny sliver. A mere fraction. [Holds up the pumpkin pie] What would you say? Would you say this pie is apple? [Puts the pie down] If I ate the whole pie, I'd hardly taste the apple. I'd only taste the pumpkin. [With knife in hand, slices remainder of apple pie] Pretty soon there will be nothing left of your race other than a handful of Americans who claim to be a fraction of who you are. And they won't be citizens of Cherokee Nation. They'll be citizens of the United States. It's inevitable. Someday, this country will lose its Indian flavor.

[He takes a bite of pie.]

SCENE 15

[*June 22, 1839. The dark of night in the Ridge Polson Cemetery. With
a shovel in hand and a kerosene lamp to light the ground,* SARAH BIRD
NORTHRUP *digs furiously.* SAMUEL WORCESTER *enters.*]

SAMUEL WORCESTER: What are you doing?

SARAH BIRD NORTHRUP: Digging.

SAMUEL WORCESTER: In the middle of the night?

SARAH BIRD NORTHRUP: I have to bury him. I have to bury him before they come back and kill all of us.

SAMUEL WORCESTER: They killed John.

SARAH BIRD NORTHRUP [*moving the lamp to reveal his bloodied body*]:
Dragged him out of bed this morning. Twelve men. Stabbed him,
who knows how many times. In our yard. In front of my children. I have children. Five children.
   Hiding in the cellar, because I am scared they are going to
come back and kill my babies. And where the hell have you been?
Where's Elias? Major Ridge? WHY AM I ALONE?

SAMUEL WORCESTER: They're dead . . . They shot the Major. He was riding horseback; they shot him as he crossed the creek into Cherokee Nation. And this morning, Elias and I were working on my roof. Two men came and asked Elias for medicine. In Cherokee.

So he got down off the roof to help them, and they—they took a hatchet to his head. Cut his skull in two. I saw it all from my roof.

SARAH BIRD NORTHRUP: My children—I have to take them away from here. I have to leave.

SAMUEL WORCESTER: Where will you go?

SARAH BIRD NORTHRUP: Arkansas?

SAMUEL WORCESTER: You should leave now. Before sunrise. So no one sees you.

[JIM ROSS *enters the cemetery, carrying* BABY RIDGE. *He stands next to* SARAH BIRD NORTHRUP.]

JIM ROSS: This here, this is your great-, great-, maybe another great-, grandfather, John Ridge—

[SARAH RIDGE POLSON *enters.*]

SARAH RIDGE POLSON: I can't find the diaper bag.

JIM ROSS: I just changed him. He's fine.

SARAH RIDGE POLSON: Oh. What are you doing?

JIM ROSS: Introducing him to his relatives.

SARAH BIRD NORTHRUP: I promised I wouldn't leave him. I told him he'd never be alone.

SAMUEL WORCESTER: Let me bury him.

[SARAH RIDGE POLSON *takes* JIM ROSS's *hand.*]

JIM ROSS [*to* BABY RIDGE]: Your grandfather, John Ridge, fought to save the sovereignty of Cherokee Nation.

SARAH BIRD NORTHRUP: Will you mark his grave?

[SAMUEL WORCESTER *nods.*]

JIM ROSS: And he won his case. In the Supreme Court. Just like your mom.

SARAH BIRD NORTHRUP: Someday, my children will return.

SARAH RIDGE POLSON [*to* BABY RIDGE]: Your name is Ridge.

SARAH BIRD NORTHRUP: I want them to find him.

[SARAH *kneels next to* JOHN's *body*].

JIM ROSS: You were born with sovereignty in your blood.

APPENDIX

Cherokee language translations created and written by John Ross (Cherokee Nation).

Page 43

MAJOR RIDGE:

We are so pleased to hear you won the election.

VG ᎣᏣᏟᎯᎵᎦ ᎣᏣᏛᎩᏍᎬ ᏣᏓᏯᎡ Ꮎ ᏓᎾᏓᏒᏰᏍᎬᎢ.

Do-yu o-tsa-li-he-li-ga o-tsa-dv-gi-sgv tsa-da-tlo-sv na da-na-da-sv-ye-sgv-i.

Page 44

MAJOR RIDGE:

We will never leave our lands.

Ꮭ ᎢᎸᎯᏳ ᏱᏓᏲᏣᏂᎩᏏ ᎦᏙ ᏙᎩᎲᎢ.

Tla i-lv-hi-yu yi-da-yo-tsa-ni-gis-si ga-do do-gi-hv-i.

Page 45

MAJOR RIDGE:

Friendship formed in danger should not be forgotten.

ᎣᎵᎢ ᏱᏄᎵᏍᏔᎾ ᎲᎦ ᎤᎾᏰᎯᏍᏗ ᎨᏒᎢ Ꮭ ᎡᎵᏍᏗ ᎢᎬᎨᏫᏍᏗ ᏱᎩ.

O-li-i yi-nu-lis-ta-na hna-yu u-na-ye-his-di ge-sv-i tla e-lis-di i-gv-ge-wis-di yi-gi.

Page 67

MAJOR RIDGE:

Making cabinets is hard, for a white man.

ᏗᏎᎯᏍᏗ ᏛᎪᏢᏍᎬ VG ᏍᏓᏯ, ᎾᏍᎩᎾᎢ ᏲᏁᎦ ᏱᎩ.

Di-se-his-di dv-go-tlv-sgv do-yu sda-ya, nas-gi-na-i yo-ne-ga yi-gi.

Page 68

MAJOR RIDGE:

There are so many things I can say in Cherokee that I cannot say in English. I refuse to limit myself.

ᏙᏳ ᎤᎪᏓ ᎪᎱᏍᏗ ᏧᏓᎴᏅᏓ ᏱᏂᏥᏫ ᏣᎳᎩ ᎬᏗ ᎾᏃ Ꮭ ᏱᏂᎨᏥᏫ ᎩᎵᏏ ᎬᏗ. ᎦᏓᏱᎭ ᎡᏍᎦ ᏯᏩᏓᏛᏗᎢ.

Do-yu u-go-da go-hv-sdi tsu-da-le-nv-da yi-ni-tsi-wi Tsa-la-gi gv-di na-no tla yi-ni-ge-tsi-wi Gi-li-si gv-di. Ga-da-yi-ha e-sga ya-wa-da-dv-di-i.

Page 69

MAJOR RIDGE:

This case isn't about a missionary. It isn't about his right to preach the Gospel on Cherokee lands against the Governor's wishes. This case is about our right to protect our citizens on our land. It's about our sovereignty.

ᎯᎠ ᎤᎾᏓᎳᏑᎸ Ꮭ ᎦᏅᏍᏟᏓ ᎨᏒᎢ ᏳᏰᎵᏓ ᏱᎩ. Ꮭ ᏳᏛᏗ ᎤᎲᎢ ᎾᏍᎩ ᎤᎵᏣᏗ ᎣᏍᏓ ᎧᏃᎮᏓ ᎤᏰᎵᏓ ᏱᎩ ᎾᎿᎢ ᏣᎳᎩ ᎦᏙ ᎤᏂᎲᎢ ᏧᎦᏘᎸᏓ Ꮎ ᏍᎦᏚᎩ ᎠᎦᏘᏯ ᎤᏚᎵᏍᎬᎩ. ᎯᎠ ᏚᎾᏓᎳᏑᎸ ᏅᏰᎵᏛ ᎾᏍᎩ ᏱᎦᏛᏁᎵᏓᏍᏗ ᎢᎩᎲ ᏗᎦᏎᏍᏙᏗ ᏗᎦᏤᎵ ᎠᏁᎯᏯ ᎤᎾᎢ ᎢᎦᏤᎵ ᎦᏙᎢ. ᎯᎠ ᎢᎩᎲ ᎢᎦᏓᏤᎵᎦᏯ ᎾᏍᎩ ᏄᏰᎵᏓ.

Hi-a u-na-da-la-su-lv tla ga-nvs-bi-da ge-sv-i yu-ye-li-da yi-gi. Tla yu-dv-di u-hv-i na-sgi u-li-tsa-di o-sda ka-no-he-da u-ye-li-da yi-gi na-hna-i Tsa-la-gi ga-do u-ni-hv-i tsu-ga-ti-lv-da na sga-du-gi a-ga-ti-ya u-du-lis-gv-gi. Hi-a du-na-da-la-su-lv nv-ye-li-dv na-sgi yi-ga-dv-ne-li-da-sdi i-gi-hv di-ga-se-sdo-di di-ga-tse-li a-ne-hi-ya u-na-i i-ga-tse-li ga-do-i. Hi-a i-gi-hv i-ga-da-tse-li-ga-ya na-sgi nu-ye-li-da.

Page 70

JOHN RIDGE:

Sovereignty is when I speak my language.

ᎾᏳᏃ ᏯᎩᏬᏂᏏ ᎠᎩᏬᏂᎯᏍᏗ ᎾᏍᎩᎾᎢ ᎤᏅᏌ ᎤᏂᎲ ᏗᎫᎪᏔᏂᏓᏍᏗ ᎨᎭᎢ.

Na-yu-no ya-gi-wo-ni-si a-gi-wo-ni-hi-sdi na-sgi-na-i u-nv-sa
u-ni-hv di-gu-go-ta-ni-da-sdi ge-so-i.

Page 71
MAJOR RIDGE:
I will escort you out.
ᏙᏯᏗᏠ ᏱᏫᎬᏯᏦᎲᎦ.
Do-ya-di-dla yi-wi-gv-ya-ka-hv-ga.

Page 111
ROGER [*telling the Cherokee creation story to* BABY RIDGE, *in Cherokee*]:
At first the earth was flat, soft, and wet. The animals grew tired of waiting.
ᎡᎶᏟ ᎠᎬᏱ ᏥᎨᏒ ᎤᏩᎾᏕᏍᎩ, ᏩᏂᎨᎢ, ᎠᎴ ᏍᏓᎵᏓ ᎨᏒᎩ.
ᎾᏍᎩᏃ ᎤᎩ ᏗᏂᎤᏌᏗ ᏍᎭᏂᏴᏓᏡ ᎠᏂᏓᏘᏴᎢ.
El-o-hi a-gv-yi tsi-ge-sv u-wa-na-de-s-gi, wa-ni-ge-i, a-le
ga-du-li-da ge-sv-gi. Na-s-gi-no nv-gi di-ni-nv-sa-di du-ni-ya-
we-tsv a-ni-ga-ti-yv-i.

Page 121
MAJOR RIDGE:
Where is the provision on jurisdiction?
ᎭᏢ ᏗᎧᎾᏩᏛᏍᏗ Ꮎ ᎠᎲ ᏗᎫᎪᏔᏂᏓᏍᏗ?
Ha-tlv di-ka-hna-wa-dv-sdi na a-hv di-gu-go-ta-ni-da-sdi?

Page 122
MAJOR RIDGE:
We discussed a representative in Congress.
ᎦᏅᏏᏛ ᏪᏕᎦᎳᏫᎩ ᎾᎿ ᎡᎳᏗ ᏗᎦᎳᏫᏍᏗ ᏩᏥᏂ ᎠᏰᎵᎢ
ᎾᏍᎩ ᎣᎩᏃᎮᎸᎢ
Ga-nv-si-dv wi-de-ga-la-wi-gi na-hna e-la-di di-ga-la-wi-sdi
wa-tsi-ni a-ye-li-i na-sgi o-gi-no-he-lv-i.

Page 123

MAJOR RIDGE:

I just signed my death warrant.

ᎠᏭᏌ ᎠᏲᎲᎯᏍᏗ ᎠᏓᏂᏴᏙᏗ ᎪᏪᎸᎦ.

A-wu-sa a-yo-hv-hi-sdi a-da-ni-yv-do-di go-we-lv-ga.

ᎤᏁᎳᏅᎯ ᎤᏪᏥ
AMAZING GRACE

ᎤᏁᎳᏅᎯ ᎤᏪᏥ	U-ne-la-nv-hi U-we-tsi
ᎢᎦᎫᏴᎮᎢ	I-ga-gu-yv-he-i
ᏂᏉ ᏦᏒ ᏫᏳᎶᏎ	Hna-quo tso-sv Wi-yu-lo-se
ᎢᎦᎫᏴᎰᏅ	I-ga-gu-yv-ho-nv.
ᎠᏎᏃ ᎢᎤᏁᏤᏱ	A-se-no I-u-ne-tse-yi
ᎢᏳᏃ ᏚᎴᏅ	I-yu-no Du-le-nv
ᏔᎵᏁ ᏛᏥᎷᏥᎵ	Ta-li-ne Dv-tsi-lu-tsi-li
ᎤᏛᏁ ᎤᏁᏨ	U-dv-ne U-ne-tsv.

God's Son
paid for us.
Then to heaven He went
after paying for us.

But He spoke
when He rose.
"I'll come again,"
He said when He spoke.